T0322794

THE GREAT BRITISH
SEWING BEE
THE TECHNIQUES

THE GREAT BRITISH
SEWING BEE
THE TECHNIQUES

All the essential tips, advice and tricks
you need to improve your sewing skills,
whatever your level

Edited by Sarah Hoggett
Photography by Clare Nicolson

quadrille

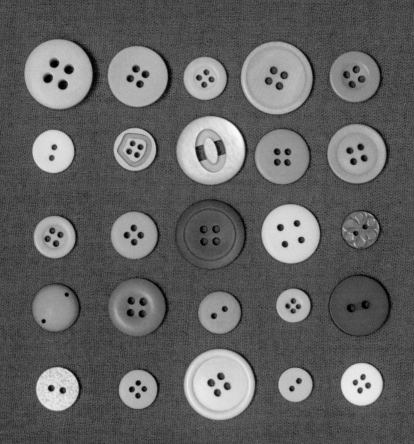

CONTENTS

6   Introduction

CHAPTER 1:
8   What do you need?
10   Basic sewing kit
16   Sewing machine

CHAPTER 2:
20   Fabrics
22   Choosing and buying fabrics
24   Woven fabrics
28   Stretch (knit) fabrics
30   Luxury fabrics
34   Fabric directory

CHAPTER 3:
38   Making clothes that fit
40   Measuring and sizing
44   Altering patterns

CHAPTER 4:
56   Get set!
58   Pretreating your fabric
60   Understanding your pattern
62   The all-important grainline
64   Lay plans
66   Pinning and cutting
68   Transferring pattern markings
70   Pattern matching
72   Interfacing

CHAPTER 5:
74   Sew simple!
76   Threading your sewing machine
78   Practice makes perfect!
79   Stitch tension
80   Pinning
81   Hand and machine stitches
84   Seams
86   Seam finishes
87   Reducing bulk
88   Hems
92   Darts
94   Zips and other fastenings
111   Sleeves
115   Sleeve finishes
119   Cuffs
122   Pockets
127   Collars
131   Facings
136   Waist finishes
142   Pleats and tucks
146   Shirring
148   Bias binding
152   Free-hanging lining

154   Glossary
157   Index
159   Acknowledgements

INTRODUCTION

Ever since *The Great British Sewing Bee* hit our TV screens for the very first time, it's become compelling viewing, not just for experienced dressmakers but also for people who've barely picked up a needle in their life. We've watched in awe as contestants craft a beautifully tailored coat or rustle up a figure-hugging dress that would grace any catwalk. We've marvelled at their ingenuity as they transform the weirdest materials – old deckchair fabric, hi-vis safety wear, you name it – into couture garments or party frocks. We've shared their frustration as invisible zips (zippers) turn out to be anything but invisible and there's no time to finish hems or sew on buttons. And we've thought, 'I'd love to have a go at that – but where do I start...?'. If you've never had the chance to learn to sew, the idea of making something that's actually good enough to wear can seem like a pipe dream.

That's where this book comes in: it brings together in one volume everything you need to know in order to start sewing simple garments for all the family. We've steered clear of complicated professional tailoring techniques – there's time to learn those when you've mastered the essentials. But we've set out all the basics in easy-to-follow steps, from choosing the right fabric to understanding a pattern, from sewing your very first seam to inserting a zip or a lining.

You may have wondered exactly what a 'sewing bee' is, so here's a brief word about the title of the programme and why it's so appropriate. Contrary to what you might expect, the 'bee' part of it doesn't refer to an insect buzzing around and being busy – it actually comes from the Old English word *bēn*, meaning a prayer, request or favour. By the late eighteenth century it had come to mean a small, informal group of people coming together to help a neighbour in need: sewing bee, quilting bee and so on. It's this community spirit that *The Great British Sewing Bee* captures so well, with contestants taking time out to advise and help their fellow competitors, even when the clock is ticking – and the moment you embark on your sewing journey, you become a part of a worldwide community of like-minded people. It doesn't really matter if your seams are a tiny bit wonky or your hems aren't perfectly level (you won't have Patrick and Esme peering over your shoulder to check!); you can take pride in the knowledge that you've made that garment yourself, from start to finish.

CHAPTER 1

What do you need?

One of the great things about dressmaking is that you don't need to spend a fortune on equipment to get started. Your biggest financial investment will be your sewing machine, but even a budget model will have all the features you need. This chapter sets out the essentials and explains what they're used for.

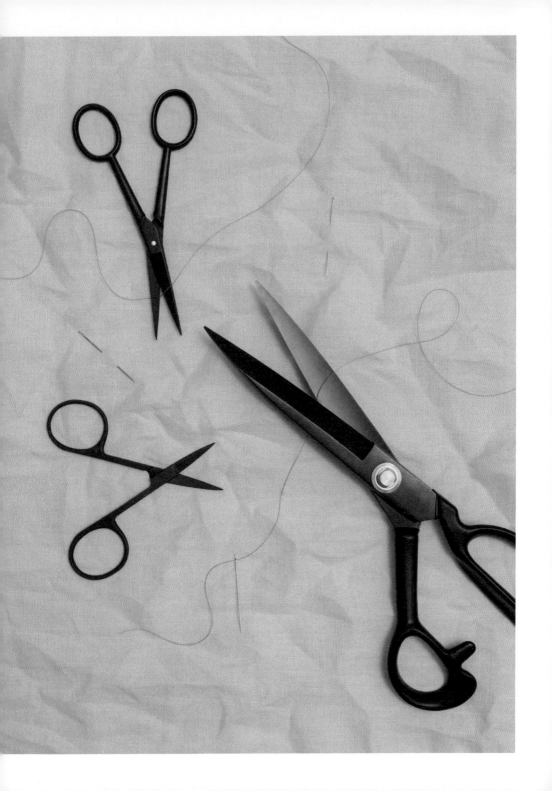

BASIC SEWING KIT

To start dressmaking, you don't need masses of tools. Here are the essentials – you've probably got some of them at home already. You can find more information on all these tools and their uses on pages 12–14.

If you're just getting started with sewing, save your pennies for beautiful fabrics; you can add more tools later on. If you are doing a technique that requires a specialist tool but you don't think you would get much use out of it in the future, see if you can borrow it from someone rather than buying it.

1. Tape measure
2. French curve and/or pattern master
3. Seam allowance gauge
4. Metre rule (not shown)
5. Tailor's chalk or dressmaker's chalk pencils
6. Dressmaker's carbon paper (not shown) and tracing wheel
7. Air- and water-soluble pens (not shown)
8. Dressmaking shears
9. Rotary cutter
10. Small scissors or snips
11. Pinking shears
12. Seam ripper
13. Paper scissors (not shown)
14. Dressmaking pins
15. Pin magnet (not shown)
16. Sewing machine needles
17. Hand sewing needles (not shown)
18. Sewing machine feet (Clockwise from the top: zipper foot, all-purpose foot, walking foot, adjustable buttonhole foot and gathering foot)
19. Sewing machine (not shown)
20. Steam iron and ironing board (not shown)
21. Pressing cloth (not shown)
22. Tailor's ham (not shown)

MEASURING TOOLS

Careful measuring is essential at every stage. In fact, the saying goes 'measure twice, cut once'!

① Tape measure

Used to measure yourself as well as your sewing projects, this is one of the most essential items in your sewing kit. A tape measure becomes less accurate over time as it stretches, so it's a good idea to replace it every once in a while.

② French curve and/or pattern master

A French curve, which is a ruler with a curved end as well as a straight edge, is used for drafting sewing patterns and adapting printed sewing patterns, particularly for grading in between sizes or trueing pattern lines (see page 44). A pattern master is extremely useful if you draft your own patterns, as it has everything you need for pattern making in one tool.

③ Seam allowance gauge

This little contraption will help you achieve perfectly even hems and seams. It's like a mini ruler with specific measurements that you can use to ensure you have an even seam allowance, a neat hem or perfectly positioned buttonholes.

④ Metre rule

A long, straight ruler is useful when creating your own patterns or straightening edges of the fabric.

MARKING TOOLS

You will need a selection of marking tools to transfer marks from patterns to fabric (see page 68). There is a large variety available, and it's very much a matter of personal preference as to which ones to use.

⑤ Tailor's chalk or dressmaker's chalk pencils

This is the traditional choice, as the marks can be easily brushed out. Both chalk slabs and pencils come in a range of colours (white, blue, yellow), so choose the one that will show up best on your fabric.

⑥ Dressmaker's carbon paper and tracing wheel

Dressmaker's carbon paper comes in a variety of colours and is used to transfer pattern outlines and indications such as darts, pleats and notches onto fabric. It is used in conjunction with a tracing wheel; you can get very spiky wheels, medium wheels and wheels with no spikes at all.

⑦ Air- and water-soluble pens

Marks made with an air-soluble pen simply disappear after a while. Water-soluble pens are a more recent innovation and have the advantage that the marks cannot be brushed off accidentally. Please note that they are only useful for marking projects that can be washed.

CUTTING TOOLS

Sharp cutting tools are essential – not only will they produce neater lines, but they will also be gentler on your hands. Look after your scissors. Blunt scissors don't achieve clean cutting lines, so make sure you sharpen them if they have reached that stage. You can have this done for you or buy a scissor sharpener.

⑧ Dressmaking shears
A pair of good-quality dressmaking shears will last you for years if you take care of them. Often they have moulded handles, so if you are left-handed, look for shears designed with you in mind. Many have angled blades so you can use them easily on a flat surface. Use dressmaking shears that are at least 20 cm (8 in.) long for cutting out your dressmaking projects.

⑨ Rotary cutter
This tool is great for cutting out fabrics that are trickier to handle, such as very fine fabrics and stretch fabrics, as you don't have to disturb the fabric once you have laid it out. Make sure your blade is sharp. You can get different sizes of blades depending on whether you are doing lots of curved lines (you will need a smaller blade) or straighter lines (you'll need a bigger blade). Always use a rotary cutter on a self-healing cutting mat.

⑩ Embroidery scissors or snips
A pair of embroidery scissors or snips is great for cutting loose thread ends, so keep them next to you as you sew.

⑪ Pinking shears
Pinking shears have zigzag edges with which to cut seam allowances and prevent them from fraying without the need for other neatening techniques. They work best on lightweight cottons and felts. However, they are not very practical: once they go blunt, you cannot sharpen them.

⑫ Seam ripper
This ultra-useful tool usually comes with your sewing machine. It may become blunt over time, so do replace it regularly. It is used to unpick seams as well as to open buttonholes.

⑬ Paper scissors
Keep a separate pair of scissors for cutting out your paper patterns. Never, ever use your dressmaking shears on paper, as they will blunt.

SEWING TOOLS

Once you're ready to start sewing, these are the tools you will need.

⑭ Dressmaking pins
Good-quality pins are a must. You have a choice of glass-headed pins, regular pins, plastic-headed pins and even novelty pins with decorative heads. Be sure to replace your pins when they become blunt or start to snag your fabrics

⑮ Pin magnet
A modern alternative to a pincushion, a pin magnet makes it easy to gather up loose pins from the floor or your work desk.

⑯ Sewing machine needles
Buy yourself a pack or two of multi-sized universal sewing machine needles to get started. For more information on different needle types and sizes, see page 19.

(17) **Hand sewing needles**
You'll need these to sew on hooks and buttons and do hand hemming. Start with a handy multi pack. These are the needles most useful for dressmaking:

Sharps – these are medium-length needles and the most popular for general hand sewing.

Betweens – these needles are shorter and are useful for quilting.

Embroidery/crewel needles – these have a longer eye, which makes them very handy for hand sewing with double or quadruple thread, such as fastenings.

Darning needles – these are generally longer, blunter needles with long eyes, used for darning but also for tacking (basting) fabrics together.

Self-threading needle – if you have difficulty threading your hand sewing needle, these ones will be your new best friends.

(18) **Sewing machine feet**
A small number of sewing machine feet – regular, zip (zipper), buttonhole – come as standard with most sewing machines. Other types that you may want to purchase as you get more experienced include an invisible zip foot, a walking foot and a gathering foot.

(19) **Sewing machine**
It goes without saying that you'll need a sewing machine. They range from simple models that do little more than straight and zigzag stitch and maybe an automatic buttonhole, to elaborate machines with lots of fancy embroidery stitches. For more information on sewing machines, see page 16.

PRESSING TOOLS

Pressing (as opposed to ironing) is essential at every stage of the dressmaking process in order to achieve a neat, professional-looking finish. Whereas ironing is the process of making a material crease free, pressing is done to ensure that all constructional seams and elements are lying flat throughout the making process, to ensure a neater finish.

(20) **Steam iron and ironing board**
A good iron with a steam button is essential for sewing: pressing in between each step, and getting crisp seams and darts, will give your makes a professional finish. Always test a swatch of your fabric with the iron to make sure you have the correct heat setting.

(21) **Pressing cloth**
This is simply a piece of folded cotton that you place in between your iron and your fabric to stop the fabric from coming into direct contact with the iron. It is particularly good for very lightweight fabrics, laces and silks, as direct contact with the hot iron can easily distort the delicate fibres.

(22) **Tailor's ham**
Pressing your garment on a tailor's ham makes it easier to press open curved seams such as sleeves,

USEFUL EXTRAS

These are not essential, but they're nice to have as part of your sewing kit.

Overlocker (serger)

An overlocker is used to finish and trim the seams of your garment, giving them a neat finish that also prevents the fabric from unravelling. However, you can also neaten seams on your sewing machine using zigzag stitch (see page 86). A three-thread overlocker is used for neatening seam allowances, whereas jersey fabrics and sportswear should be sewn on a four-thread overlocker for extra strength.

Bias tape maker

Making bias binding is so much easier with the use of a tape maker (see page 151). They are available in different sizes or widths to create bias binding ranging from 6 mm (¼ in.) to 5 cm (2 in.). Generally, the width of the strip is twice the finished folded binding – so if you want 2.5 cm (1 in.) wide bias binding, cut strips to 5 cm (2 in.).

Point turner

This little tool helps achieve crisp corners. It has a point at one end for pushing out corners fully and often also has measurements marked on one side that can be used to measure and mark hem allowance and depth of pleats. If you don't have a point turner, use a knitting needle instead.

Pattern weights

Pattern weights hold down your fabric and pattern, and are a quicker and easier solution than pinning. They are great to use on delicate fabrics such as silk if you want to avoid pin marks and they work well with stretch fabrics such as jerseys if you are using a rotary cutter to cut out. Weights are not suitable if you are going to use scissors.

Pattern paper

Essential when creating your own patterns, making adjustments to existing patterns or tracing off designs. You can choose dot-and-cross, plain or gridded paper. The gridded or dot-and-cross versions help to ensure straight of grain, while the plain paper is easier to see through.

SEWING MACHINE

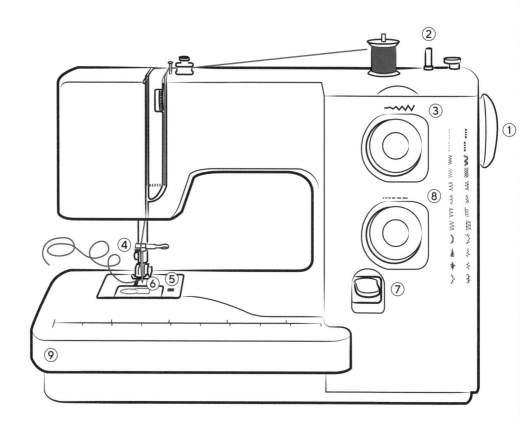

THE ANATOMY OF A SEWING MACHINE

All sewing machines work in basically the same way. They have a top thread and a bobbin thread, which interlock to create the stitching visible on the top and bottom of the fabric. All sewing machines also have the basic components in the same place.

KEY

① Balance wheel
② Bobbin winding spindle
③ Tension dial
④ Needle
⑤ Throat plate
⑥ Feed dogs
⑦ Reverse stitch lever/button
⑧ Stitch width and stitch length dials/buttons
⑨ Flat bed/ free arm

① Balance wheel

Found on the upper right side of the machine, the balance wheel is used to lower and raise the needle by hand. Always turn the wheel towards yourself. On older or cheaper models of machine, there may be a separate outer ring that is pulled out a little to disengage the needle when winding bobbins.

② Bobbin winding spindle

To wind a bobbin, place it on the winding spindle and thread, following the bobbin thread path. Most bobbins will only wind until they are full and then automatically stop. The thread on the bobbin should feel firm and look evenly wound.

Bobbin – your machine may have a drop-in or a front entry bobbin that sits in its own case. Drop in the bobbin with the thread coming off correctly, from left to right (anti- or counterclockwise). If the bobbin is inserted the other way, with the thread coming off clockwise, it may cause skipped stitches.

For front-loading bobbins, insert the full bobbin with the thread coming off clockwise. Pull the thread end through the gap in the casing to pull it through the bobbin tension and then insert the casing into the front of the machine.

③ Tension dial

The thread and needle tension is set by a dial on the front or top of the machine, normally just above the needle area. It is numbered and will usually have the most common or default tension highlighted in some way – by darker numbers or circled numbers. Generally, leave the tension set at the default position as most modern machines stitch perfectly well on all types of fabric. If you do adjust the tension, do so a little at a time. Perfect stitches are formed

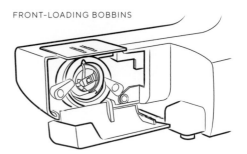

FRONT-LOADING BOBBINS

when the top thread is visible only on the top of the fabric, and the bobbin thread only on the underside.

④ Needle

Machine needles have a flat section on the shank, which is usually placed 'flat to back' of the machine when fitted up into the needle socket. Tighten the screw holding the needle in place with a screwdriver (this is one of the tools that's normally provided when you buy a new machine) to prevent it working loose as you sew.

⑤ Throat plate

This has markings to show different seam allowances, as well as the central holes through which the feed dogs rotate and the needle goes to pick up the bobbin thread.

⑥ Feed dogs

Under and protruding through the throat plate are the feed dogs – the gripper teeth that rotate to help move on the fabric under the presser foot as it is stitched.

⑦ Reverse stitch lever/button

All machines will have a reverse stitch lever or button on the front of the machine; most have to be held down to continue stitching in reverse and, when released, will then revert to forward stitching.

⑧ **Stitch width and stitch length dials/buttons**

These are used to alter the width and length of the selected stitch. A standard length for most purposes is 2.2 to 2.5. Use a longer stitch for multi-layers or bulky fabrics. Stitch width is used for all sideways stitches (zigzag or decorative stitches). The higher the number or wider the printed scale, the longer or wider the stitch.

⑨ **Flat bed/free arm**

All machines have a 'flat bed' – the surface area around the needle that helps to hold fabric flat as it is sewn. Most convert to 'free arm' by taking part of the flat bed away. The part that can be removed may be clipped to the front, the back or wrapped around front, back and side. It frequently holds the tools tray too. Converting to free arm gives you a narrow section that extends above the worktop, which means you can stitch small areas such as cuffs, sleeves and trouser (pants) legs more easily.

ADDED EXTRAS

As machines increase in price, so they increase in functions and facilities. Many of the additional features are conveniently sited just above the needle area, so they are close to hand when you are sewing. These can include a fix/lock stitch button, a sewing speed lever, a stop/start button to use instead of a foot pedal and a knee lift lever.

MACHINE MAINTENANCE

A little bit of regular maintenance will keep your sewing machine running smoothly.

- When you buy a machine, it usually comes with a small box of accessories containing all the cleaning equipment you need, such as oil, screwdrivers and a tiny lint cleaning brush. A pair of tweezers is also useful.

- When you're not using your machine, cover it up so as not to attract dust.

- Before you embark on any cleaning and maintenance, unplug the machine from the power supply.

- Defluff the machine after every project by removing the bobbin and using the small lint brush that comes with the machine to brush off any lint from the thread guides and in and around the bobbin case. Then remove lint and thread from the feed dogs and the back of the needle plate. Use tweezers to gently tease out any lint or threads that are jammed in tight. Occasionally you should also unscrew and remove the throat plate, remove the bobbin holder and brush out underneath.

- Some people suggest using cans of compressed air to blow dust and lint from moving parts, but this can blow material deeper into your machine, causing long-term damage; a small brush is best.

- Many modern sewing machines are self-lubricating so you don't need to oil them. However, they do still need regular maintenance and servicing.

SEWING MACHINE NEEDLES

There are many different types and sizes of sewing machine needles you will need in your sewing kit. The chart on the right will help you choose the right size of sewing machine needle for your fabric. Needles for domestic sewing machines are universal, meaning they will fit any sewing machine brand. You will need different kinds of needles for industrial sewing machines, and also different needles for overlockers (sergers). In addition to the different sizes of needles in the chart, you might also need to use a ballpoint needle for stretch fabrics, a twin needle for decorative topstitching or finishing hems on knit fabrics, and a topstitching needle.

....

TOP TIP

Change your sewing machine needle after every eight hours of sewing, or after every project – particularly if you're sewing tough fabrics or multi-layers. If your needle is blunt, it won't stitch as neatly.

....

American needle size	European needle size	Fabric weight	Fabric types
8	60	Very fine	Fine silk, chiffon, organza, voile, fine lace
9	65	Very fine	Fine silk, chiffon, organza, voile, fine lace
10	70	Very fine	Fine silk, chiffon, organza, voile, fine lace
11	75	Light-weight	Cotton voile, silk, muslin, spandex, Lycra
12	80	Standard	Cotton, synthetics, spandex, Lycra
14	90	Medium-weight	Denim, corduroy, multiple layers
16	100	Heavy-weight	Heavy denim, heavy corduroy, leather
18	110	Very heavy	Upholstery fabric, leather
20	120	Extra heavy	Heavy upholstery fabric, thick leather, vinyl

CHAPTER 2

Fabrics

One of the pleasures of dressmaking is that you get to choose the fabrics and colours you want to wear – but of course, it can be a little daunting if you don't know what type of fabric to use for a particular garment or whether any special sewing techniques are needed. Here's a basic guide to different fabric types, with tips on how to sew them successfully.

CHOOSING AND BUYING FABRICS

With so many fabrics to choose from, how do you decide which one to buy? A commercial pattern will feature a list of suggested fabrics, as well of details of how much fabric you need to buy for your size, but even that can be quite bewildering if you're new to sewing. Start by asking yourself a few simple questions:

WHAT FABRICS DO I LIKE?

Go to your wardrobe and find a similar garment to the one you are making. What does the fabric feel like? Is it floaty or sturdy? Learn what your favourite garments are made of and take it from there.

WHAT LOOK AM I GOING FOR?

Many garments can be made in different fabrics, depending on the look you are going for: a silk blouse, for example, has a more dressed-up look than a cotton or linen blouse. So think about how and when you will wear the garment.

HOW DOES THE FABRIC DRAPE?

'Drape' simply means the way the fabric falls in folds. Do you want a skirt to fall in graceful folds or to have crisp, sharp pleats? Do you want a dress to hug your figure or skim over the curves? A fabric with high drape will be flowy, meaning that it hangs in small creases and clings; silk, satin and chiffon usually have high drape. A fabric with low drape is stiffer and holds its shape more; heavy cotton, denim and corduroy all have low drape. To test the way a fabric drapes, simply place a piece of fabric on top of your arm or another surface to see how it looks when it falls.

WHAT'S MY SEWING SKILL LEVEL?

Woven fabrics such as cottons are recommended for beginners as they're easy to sew with and you don't need special techniques. Stretch fabrics require slightly different tools and techniques, but medium-weight stretch materials are great for all levels of ability. Some fabrics, such as fine silks or faux suede, can be tricky to handle unless you're quite an experienced dressmaker, so bear that in mind.

WHERE CAN I SHOP?

A good fabric store is like an Aladdin's cave, piled high with bolts of fabric in different colours, patterns, weights and fibres. If you're lucky enough to have a local shop where you can actually see and feel the fabric for yourself before you buy, that's great – but not all of us are that fortunate. Thankfully, online fabric stores have improved immeasurably in recent years and have managed to take a lot of the guesswork out of buying. They also offer you the chance to buy fabrics from all over the world that bricks-and-mortar shops simply wouldn't have the space to stock. Refer to our top tips (see right) for buying online.

MAKING SENSE OF FABRIC WIDTHS

Most fabrics come woven in widths between 110 and 150 cm (44 and 60 in.), but in reality the 110-cm (44-in.) widths are not very suitable for dressmaking. This width is often used in quilting cottons and is often too narrow for your pattern pieces, especially once the fabric has been folded in half. Selecting a width of between 130 and 150 cm (50 and 60 in.) ensures that you can cut most pattern pieces out and you don't have any issues cutting on the fold. You can also choose to not cut on the fold, although this is usually only economical in wider widths.

STILL CONFUSED?

Over the next few pages, you'll learn more about how fabric is produced and different fabric types. There's also a Fabric Directory (page 34), which gives brief descriptions of many of the most popular fabrics for dressmaking and the kind of garments they're most suited to.

TIPS

° Sign up for online store newsletters so that you find out about special offers as soon as they're available.

° Most online fabric stores will send samples so that you can feel the weight of the fabric, match the colours to your project and check the drape. Some offer a free sample service while others have a minimal charge to cover postage or allow you to redeem the cost of samples against a future purchase.

° Check whether the fabric is sold by the metre or some other unit. With some stores the price you're quoted is for half a metre, so if you want a whole metre of fabric you'll need to buy two units.

° Check the fabric width, too, to make sure you're buying the amount you need – and remember that you may need to buy more if you're using a napped fabric, a one-directional print or a large-patterned fabric (see page 65).

° If you're not sure whether a particular fabric is right for your project, contact the retailer and ask for more information.

° Find out what the shipping costs are – otherwise that gorgeous fabric that you found on special offer may not be as much of a bargain as you thought.

° Can you cut down on shipping costs by increasing the size of your order? If you regularly use a particular kind of interfacing or thread, for example, it's worth stocking up before you run out and that might be enough to tip you into the free shipping category.

WOVEN FABRICS

Woven fabrics are made up of warp threads (going down the length of the fabric) and weft threads (going across the width). Woven fabric can be light- or heavyweight, depending on the yarn used.

The way the yarn is handled as it's woven dictates what type of cloth is produced. Many of the most popular fabrics for dressmaking are woven; there are three main types:

PLAIN WEAVE (1)

This is the most readily available and popular type of woven fabric. The fabric is woven with long warp threads along the length of the cloth, and weft threads evenly interlaced across the width of the cloth. Plain-weave fabrics are usually very easy to sew, gather and handle.

TWILL WEAVE (2)

This type of weave creates the most durable cloths like gabardine, denim and chino. The weft threads don't weave in an even pattern horizontally across the warp threads. Instead, they create a series of over-and-under sequences, changing with each row and building a diagonal pattern. The diagonal pattern appears in the cloth like ridges and is particularly noticeable in denim. It's possible to vary the over-under sequence to create different patterns, such as a herringbone effect.

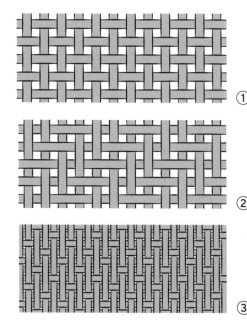

SATIN WEAVE (3)

This is the least durable woven cloth, but it creates wonderful special-occasion fabrics. The weft threads are woven with long spaces or 'floats' across the warp threads. It's these floats that attract light and create the satin quality. Satin weaving enables elaborate patterns to be woven. Damask and jacquard weaving are both types of satin woven fabrics.

COTTON

Cotton is the best choice for anyone who is new to sewing, and yet there are enough variations of cotton cloth to afford endless possibilities for even an experienced dressmaker. Cotton can be blended with many other fibres, which is one of the reasons why it's so versatile. It's often blended with other natural fibres, such as silk or linen, as well as with advanced technological fibres that create specific properties – to make a non-iron fabric for shirts, for instance.

EXAMPLES OF COTTON FABRICS:

Batiste, chambray, cheesecloth, corduroy, denim, drill (also called chino), eyelet (also called broderie anglaise), flannelette, gingham, lawn, moleskin, muslin, poplin, sateen, shirting cottons.

Polycotton (a blend of polyester and cotton, sometimes 50:50 but often 65% cotton and 35% polyester) and silk-cotton mixes, which combine a cotton weave with the lustre and drape of silk, are also popular.

LINEN

Linen is spun from the long, waxy fibres of the flax plant. It has a natural lustre and three times the strength of cotton. It doesn't take dye as well as cotton, which results in richer, plain colours where the pattern is generally woven into rather than printed onto the fabric. Because it creases easily, people either love or avoid linen. On the plus side, linen presses beautifully and looks sophisticated, while lining and interlinings can help reduce creasing in the finished garment. Linen keeps you cooler than cotton because of its breath-ability and ability to wick away moisture, so it's an excellent fabric for summer.

....

WORKING WITH COTTON AND LINEN

- Use a needle size that's appropriate to the fabric weight, from fine 65/9 needles for lightweight cotton fabrics to 100/16 for denim, corduroy or thick layers (see page 19). Keep a selection of 65/9–80/12 needles in your workbox.

....

WOOL

Wool is available in many fabric weights, textures and qualities, from floaty gossamer sheers to heavy blanket-weight plaids. As it's an excellent insulator, it will keep you warm in winter and cool in the summer. Wool is naturally water repellent and has some natural flame-resistant properties, making it a great choice for outerwear.

There are two distinct types of wool yarns, producing two types of woollen fabric: **woollen yarn**, which is produced when the fleece has been carded and then drawn prior to spinning, and **worsted yarn**, which is carded, drawn and then combed prior to spinning. Both types of woollen yarns can be used to create either woven or knitted fabrics, and wool is often blended with man-made fibres to create more technical fabrics.

Woollen spun fabric feels soft, with a coarse surface texture. Woollen fabrics are easier to sew with and less expensive than a worsted fabric. This type of wool is not ideal for elegant or fine tailoring, as it doesn't hold its shape as well as a worsted fabric, but it's great for more casual garments and coats.

Worsted spun fabric has a smother, flatter and more lustrous appearance than woollen fabric. It is used to make finer, smooth-surfaced fabrics such as twill, gabardine and suiting. Worsted fabrics are considered the ultimate fabric for elegant tailoring.

EXAMPLES OF WOOL FABRICS:

Boiled wool, bouclé, cashmere, challis, crepe, flannel, gabardine, houndstooth, melton, tartan, tweed.

WORKING WITH WOOL

- Wool fabric can shrink. Unless you buy pre-shrunk wool (called needle ready), steam it well before cutting.
- To work out which is the fabric's right side, look for the smoother selvedge. Mark the wrong side with crosses in tailor's chalk so that you don't get confused later.
- Always cut out with a nap layout (see page 65).
- Use tailor's tacks (see page 69) to transfer markings, as chalk and carbon paper can fall off the surface of the cloth.
- Use a seam roll when pressing seams in heavier wool fabric to avoid getting imprints on the right side.
- Always let the area you've pressed cool down before moving it off the ironing board; this allows the press to set.
- Twill woven fabrics such as gabardine are prone to shine when pressed, so always test and use a pressing cloth.
- For loosely woven woollens such as bouclé, use a walking foot that doesn't slide the two layers of fabric together as you sew.
- Practise seams on a double layer of fabric before sewing – you'll need longer stitches for really thick wool.

SILK

Silk has a lustrous, shimmering quality due to the unique structure of silk fibres, which can reflect light like a triangular prism. Silk feels cool in summer and warm in winter. Because it's lightweight and can resist wrinkling, it's an excellent fabric choice for travelling clothes. Silk is the strongest natural fibre. However, its slipperiness makes it difficult to handle. It can all too easily slither around as you machine stitch it, resulting in inaccurate seam matching, puckers and bubbles or, worse, the fabric getting caught and damaged in the feed dogs.

Silk is now woven and knitted into all types of cloth, so it is no longer exclusively reserved for lingerie. Blended with wool, cotton or technical fibres, silk can be made into any kind of cloth, from chiffon to tweed to charmeuse.

EXAMPLES OF SILK FABRICS:

Charmeuse, crepe de Chine, dupion, habotai, noil, tussah.

WORKING WITH SILK

- If you've never sewn with silk before, try using a silk blend or a firmer weight of silk rather than a sheer chiffon.
- The sheen on silk is similar to a nap, so cut out using a nap layout (see page 65).
- If you are using a slippery silk, cut out in single layers only (see page 66).
- If your fabric is very slippery and won't lie still, place it on top of some tissue paper and treat the tissue paper as part of the fabric: pin the pattern pieces to it, cut out fabric and paper together, and sew with the tissue paper on the bottom. This gives the machine something to grip; you can tear the paper out of the seam afterwards.
- Avoid using wax or vanishing markers on silk, as they can leave a residue that's impossible to get out.
- Pins can easily mark the fabric. Use bridal or lace pins, which are extra fine, and pin within the seam allowances rather than within the pattern lines. Alternatively, weight the pattern pieces.
- Lots of silk fabric watermarks, so test press before using your iron on the fabric to avoid spotting.
- Use a small needle size (60 or 70/8 or 10), lower your stitch length to between 2.2 and 2.5 to avoid puckering and select a fine thread such as a polyester.
- Hand tack (baste) seams for fitting to avoid making permanent holes from machine stitching.
- Avoid the sewing machine needle sucking in the fabric at the start of seams by using a 'stitch starter': double fold a piece of thicker cloth and start sewing on that before continuing onto your seam.

STRETCH (KNIT) FABRICS

Stretch (knit) fabrics are created by interlocking yarn around needles, creating looped stitches. It's the looping of the yarn that creates the elasticity or stretch in the fabric, rather than the fibre content of the yarn itself: it's possible to buy cotton, wool, silk and synthetic fibres in knits, and there are also blended knit fabrics.

While all knitted fabrics have some stretch, the amount and direction of stretch vary considerably depending on the way the fabric is knitted and the type of yarn used.

WARP KNIT (1)

A warp knit is made by multiple needles moving up and down, with each needle forming one loop arranged in parallel vertical columns. Warp knits have little or no vertical stretch and varying degrees of crossways stretch.

WEFT KNIT (2)

A weft knit is made with a single yarn that's looped to create horizontal rows, with each row built on the previous row. Weft knits have moderate to high crossways stretch and some lengthways stretch; they are more prone to shrinkage and losing their shape.

Stretch fabrics come in all weights and qualities, from fine stretchy underwear to sweatshirts, fleece and even faux fur. Just like woven fabrics, some are easier to sew than others. If you've never used knit fabric before, start with a stable double knit such as a ponte de Roma or a cotton interlock fabric.

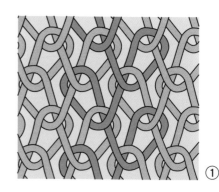

EXAMPLES OF STRETCH FABRICS:

Double knit, fleece, four-way stretch, interlock, jersey, rib knit, spandex and Lycra, sweatshirt knit, two-way stretch.

WORKING WITH STRETCH FABRICS

- With such a range of weights and qualities, sew test seams each time you use a new knit fabric. Keep a notebook with samples and the settings you find work best. Narrow zigzag is a great choice for seaming knits on a regular machine.

- Use a ballpoint or stretch needle in your machine. These specialist needles have rounded points, so they will separate the fibres in your fabric rather than piercing them, which could create laddering.

- Lay the pattern correctly across the direction of stretch. Knits have more stretch across the width, which is best laid around the body.

- Use a nap layout when cutting out (see page 65).

- Stitching a stretchy fabric with a straight stitch can result in broken stitches when the garment is pulled on or off. Choose a stretch stitch (consult your sewing machine manual) or a small zigzag stitch, reduced to 2.5 width, stretching the fabric slightly as you sew.

- Stretch fabric can easily distort out of shape when made up, so think about stabilizing shoulder seams and finished edges by adding a strip of fusible stabilizer tape (ease tape) to the seam allowance. Use a knit stabilizer that's a similar weight to your fabric.

- Decrease the pressure on your sewing foot if your machine has that function. This can stop the fabric from stretching out as it's sewn and fluting.

- When sewing with an overlocker (serger), adjust the differential feed to avoid fluted seams. Test that the needle tension is high enough so the threads don't show when the seam is stretched open.

- Not all knitted fabrics will fray, so you often won't need to neaten your raw edges. Test the edge of a piece to see if your fabric frays.

- The edges of knit fabric can have a tendency to curl, causing bulky seams. To avoid this, stitch a double seam by stitching two parallel rows close together, working both in the same direction. Stitch the first row using a stretch or zigzag stitch. Stitch again in the seam allowance a scant 3 mm (⅛ in.) away, using either a straight or a small zigzag stitch, then trim close to the stitching.

LUXURY FABRICS

Luxury fabrics come in all fibres, types and qualities, but what makes them special is how they drape, feel and look. They are not the first choice for anyone new to sewing, but with a little practice they are really worth the effort. Most luxury fabrics are more expensive than everyday fabrics, as they're created in more labour-intensive ways.

LACE

Lace was originally hand made using a series of intertwined threads and bobbins or by embroidering a fine cloth. Most modern lace is now made by machine. Lace never seems to go out of fashion, whether it's white lace for summer or jewel colours for the festive party season. It is a romantic, pretty fabric, which makes it a perennially popular choice for wedding gowns.

Lace is produced either as a fabric or as narrow trim known as an insertion. Using a lace insertion is a cost-effective way to add a touch of luxury to a garment. While it's true that lace is delicate and needs careful handling when sewn, it's actually more forgiving than you might expect, and mistakes can often be disguised.

EXAMPLES OF LACE FABRICS:

Alencon lace, Chantilly lace, Guipure lace, metallic lace.

WORKING WITH LACE

° Avoid using a heavily corded lace for your first lace project as it's trickier to sew with. An all-over lace with no large spaces is a great first choice.

° If you're using a large-patterned lace, buy an extra 75 cm (30 in.) or so to allow for matching up.

° Lace often has a one-way design, so cut it out in a single layer (see page 66).

° Consider where to place the motifs in the lace pattern on your garment – make sure you centre motifs on garment pieces, for example. You'll also need to match up the lace pattern horizontally.

° Do a test press on a scrap of lace to work out the temperature. Start with a synthetic setting, as often lace fabric is blended with synthetic fibres. Use a press cloth to avoid the lace melting.

° Tailor's tacks are the best way to transfer pattern markings; chalk and dressmaker's carbon paper marks just don't stay on.

SHEERS

Sheer fabrics really are the ultimate luxury fabric. Many sheer fabrics were originally only available in silk, making them costly, but the development of synthetic fibres means that less expensive, good-quality, man-made sheer fabrics are now readily available.

Sheer fabric falls into three main groups – crisp, semi-crisp and soft. All three groups have fabrics made up of many different fibres, weights and qualities. It's possible to have woven or knitted sheer fabric, and the amount of transparency also varies greatly.

Sheer fabric is definitely not the best choice for your first-ever sewing project. The sheerness of the fabric means seams and hems are all very visible, so you should really feel comfortable using a machine before tackling these lovely fabrics. If you've never sewn with sheer fabric before, try sewing a crisp or semi-crisp weight first. The hardest types of sheer to sew are the slippery, soft fabrics such as chiffon or georgette. Net fabrics like tulle also fall into the category of sheer, although they're more robust and easier to sew.

EXAMPLES OF SHEER FABRICS:

Chiffon, gauze, georgette, net, organdie, organza, tulle, voile.

WORKING WITH SHEERS

- If the fabric is slippery when cutting, try weighting the pattern in place and using a rotary cutter and mat. Alternatively, use a really sharp pair of serrated shears.

- Don't transfer pattern markings with carbon paper – this may mark the fabric.

- Use fine dressmaking pins and change your machine needle to a fresh fine one.

- It can help to reduce the foot pressure on your machine if that function is available.

- Always do a test seam and a test press. Start with a low temperature and avoid prolonged exposure to the iron if you want to avoid scorching.

- Sheer fabrics are generally very lightweight, so be sure to use light closures – featherweight zips (zippers) and tiny buttons and hooks.

SATIN AND TAFFETA

Both satin and taffeta have a lustrous sheen and are suitable for all types of elegant evening or bridal wear.

Satin is available in all fibres from cotton to silk and polyester. It's the satin weave of the fabric itself that gives the cloth its distinctive surface sheen, rather than the fibre content. It's available in all weights from a slinky charmeuse to heavy double-faced satin and duchesse satin. Satin seams can creep when sewn, so choose patterns without lots of seaming and details. The surface has a pile-like quality that is easily crushed when ironed.

Taffeta is a fine, crisp fabric with a paper-like quality that rustles when worn. A rib weave fabric, it is densely woven yet light. Originally made from silk, it's now readily available in polyester, acetate or nylon.

EXAMPLES OF SATIN AND TAFFETA:

Crepe-backed satin, duchesse satin, moiré taffeta, satin brocade, shot taffeta, tissue or paper taffeta.,   .

WORKING WITH SATIN AND TAFFETA

° Store satin fabric rolled to avoid bruising the surface.

° Before sewing, make sure your workspace is clean and wash your hands to remove any oil residue. If your cutting table has a rough surface, cover it with an oilcloth.

° Use a nap layout (see page 65) when cutting satin fabric.

° Don't transfer pattern markings with a tracing wheel, as this may mark the fabric.

° Hand tack (baste) seams before fitting, as machine needles damage the fabric.

° Always do some test seams to work out the best settings, and start with a new fine sewing-machine needle.

SEQUINNED FABRICS

Sequinned fabrics add a definite touch of 'bling' to special-occasion wear, but sewing them requires a few specialist techniques. They're not a good choice for beginners!

WORKING WITH SEQUINNED FABRICS

- Use a nap layout (see page 65) when cutting out.

- Cut from a single layer of fabric (see page 66), with the fabric right side up.

- Change the needle frequently, as it will blunt more easily.

- Use sew-in interfacings where interfacing is necessary (see page 72). Alternatively, use a transparent organza as an interfacing so that it doesn't change the look or handle of the garment.

- Press with care from the wrong side, with a press cloth covering the material.

- Avoid using steam on sequinned fabrics as it might tarnish the sequins.

- When handling the cut pieces, if the sequins or beads are dropping from the edges, apply drafting tape to the cut edge temporarily until the seams are stitched.

- Sew with straight seams, using machine needle size 60–75 (9–11) depending on the base fabric with a stitch length of 2.2–2.5.

- Remove sequins and beads from seam allowances by carefully cutting away individual sequins. Do not cut the threads holding them in place, as this may unravel more than you wanted to remove. (1)

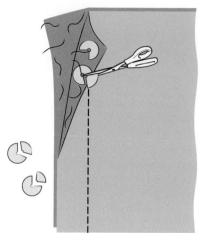

FABRIC DIRECTORY

This is by no means an exhaustive list of all the fabrics available, but it covers the majority of non-specialist fabrics that you're likely to come across and gives an indication of what you can use them for.

Acetate: A silky synthetic fabric with excellent draping qualities, acetate is most commonly used for garment linings.

Alençon lace: A French needlepoint lace with a delicate floral pattern on a net background.

Batiste: A plain-woven fabric that is similar to lawn, although slightly heavier, available in varying degrees of sheerness.

Boiled wool: Often confused with felt, this is knitted wool that has been shrunk and felted. It still retains a little of its stretch and has a distinctive textured surface. Available in varying weights, it's good for unstructured jackets, coats, dresses and skirts.

Bouclé: A loosely woven, textured woollen fabric that has distinctive loops and curls over the surface. Use for casual drapey jackets, dresses and skirts.

Cashmere: This super-soft, luxurious cloth is usually blended with wool to make it affordable. It makes wonderful coats and jackets, but can be made into almost any garment depending on the weight.

Challis: This is a soft, lightweight wool often used for paisley scarves. It drapes beautifully and comes in varying weights, including sheer. Use it for winter blouses and dresses.

Chambray: A soft cotton fabric in which the vertical threads are coloured and the horizontal threads are white, creating its distinctive sheen and iridescent effect. It launders well and is easy to sew with. Use a lightweight version for shirts, dresses and children's clothes. The heavier-weight cloth makes excellent shorts and trousers (pants).

Chantilly lace: A pretty, very fine French lace characterized by the fringed quality of the scalloped edges. This lace is very fine and needs to be cut and sewn with care.

Charmeuse: This gorgeous silk drapes beautifully. Also known as silk satin, it has a lustrous glossy sheen on one side, with a matt look on the reverse and is available in varying weights and qualities. Use it to make exceptional lingerie, blouses and special-occasion wear.

Chiffon: Available in many fibres, silk is the most luxurious of the chiffons. Chiffon is soft and slippery and is one of the most tricky fabrics to sew. Use it to make blouses, full skirts and lingerie.

Corduroy: Corduroy piles come in various widths, from fine (needle) to large (elephant). Choose a lighter, narrow-ribbed cord for shirts and dresses and use thicker-ribbed corduroy for dungarees, trousers (pants) and jackets.

Crepe: This fabric has a slightly crinkled surface that's formed by twisted yarns with a crepe weave. Wool crepe has a wonderful drape, making it perfect for dresses and blouses. It's available in light to mid weights. Crepe is also available in many other fibres, so it's possible to buy crepe fabric as almost any type of cloth.

Crepe-backed satin: This fabric is reversible, with a shiny satin side and a matt crepe side on the reverse. It's available in various weights and is often used to create stunning gowns utilizing both sides of the fabric.

Crepe chiffon: Similar to chiffon, this has all the properties of crepe but in a sheer. Harder to sew than chiffon, it's used for special-occasion wear.

Crepe de Chine: A light- to medium-weight silk fabric woven with crepe yarns, which give it a slightly crinkled texture, crepe de Chine drapes wonderfully. The crepe surface means that it's less glossy than other silks. Use it to make blouses, scarves and evening wear.

Denim: A densely woven cotton. Traditionally blue warp threads are twill woven with undyed weft threads, although denim can be produced in colours other than indigo and is now available in many weights. Use a denim needle for heavier-weight denim.

Double knit: Double knit is a firm, stable, knit with little stretch, characterized by vertical rows of ribs on either side of the fabric. It's available in all weights and qualities and can be produced in lots of fibres. Double knits are great for structured garments that don't need a lot of stretch; use them to make structured dresses, skirts, tops, and trousers (pants).

Drill: A dense twill weave, this is a durable, hardwearing cotton fabric with a diagonal ribbed effect. It is similar to denim and can be dyed in all colours. It makes great trousers (pants), structured skirts and jackets.

Duchesse satin: An elegant and very lustrous fabric, which is heavier than a charmeuse. It drapes beautifully. Use it for really special evening wear or bridal clothes.

Dupion: Also known as Indian silk, dupion has a distinctive slubs in the weave. Dupion is woven from silk that's come from double cocoons, where two silkworms have spun close together. A crisp, medium-weight silk that's woven in myriad colours, it's often shot with a second colour. Relatively inexpensive, it's popular for evening gowns and bridal wear.

Eyelet (also known as broderie anglaise): This is a lacy cotton fabric that's perfect for summer tops, dresses and blouses. The base fabric is usually a lightweight lawn, batiste or voile that has been embroidered with decorative holes or eyelets. As the fabric is sheer with holes, consider underlining or lining any garments made with eyelet.

Flannel: Used in suits and tailoring, flannel is usually a plain or twill weave cloth, with a soft, dull, surface texture and a slight nap. Use the lighter weights for shirts and dressing gowns and medium weights for suits and dresses.

Flannelette: This comes in many weights and can be made from fibres other than cotton. The fabric is a loose weave that has a nap on the right side. Cotton flannel is often called 'brushed cotton'. Use it to make cosy nightwear and children's clothes.

Fleece: Made from synthetic polyester fibres that have been shrunk and then felted, fleece is a dense fabric with a soft, fluffy pile. It's available in different weights and qualities and is fairly easy to sew. It's the perfect fabric for children's wear, sweatshirts and soft jackets.

Four-way stretch: These are fabrics that stretch across both the width and length of the fabric. This type of stretch fabric has better recovery than other knit fabrics and is often used for sports clothes. Available in many weights and qualities, it is often produced from synthetic or man-made fibres.

Gabardine: A classic suiting fabric, gabardine is a woollen twill weave with a distinctive ribbed pattern and a slight sheen. Use it for suits and dresses. Gabardine is also made from cotton and commonly used for raincoats.

Georgette: Georgette can look like chiffon, but has a looser weave and a slightly rougher texture. It is usually made from polyester blends or silk and sews up more easily than chiffon. It's perfect for blouses and lingerie.

Gingham: This firmly woven cotton is best known for its characteristic checked design; the checked pattern is woven in rather than printed and ranges from teeny checks to large bold ones. Use lighter weights for summer tops and blouse and heavier weights for trousers (pants), shorts and structured skirts.

Guipure lace: Sometimes known as Venetian lace, this sturdy lace does not feature a net background. The design is embroidered with cotton fibres onto a dissolvable background.

Habotai: A Japanese silk that's soft, light and crisp, habotai is a plain weave and is an excellent fabric for anyone new to sewing silk. Use it to make blouses, shirts or as a lining.

Houndstooth: A woollen fabric woven with two colours and with a distinctive broken checked pattern. The smaller patterns are called 'dog tooth'. Houndstooth is available in many weights and is suitable for outerwear, suits or dresses, depending on the weight.

Interlock: This stretch knit is often made from cotton and used to make T-shirts. Interlock is soft, drapes well and is characterized by fine lengthwise ribs on both sides of the fabric.

Jersey: Jersey is a stable, drapey knit with limited stretch. Single-knit jersey has lengthwise fine ribs on one side with purl knit on the other side. Double-knit jersey has lengthwise ribs on both sides. Use it to make wrap dresses, tops, skirts and drapey trousers (pants).

Lawn: A lightweight cotton fabric with lovely drape, lawn has a slight sheen and a semi-crisp quality. It's a great choice for summer dresses, children's clothes and blouses.

Melton: This heavyweight woollen twill weave is used for outerwear. The fabric appears felted due to its brushed texture.

Metallic lace: This can be made as any type of lace that has metallic threads in the pattern of the lace.

Moiré taffeta: This fabric has a distinctive water-marked pattern that looks like the rippling surface of water. Available in various weights, it's often used for the lapels of tuxedos and to make coats and jackets.

Muslin: A light, plain-weave cotton fabric that is usually sold in its unbleached state and is often used to make toiles.

Net: Made from many fibres, but usually man made, net comes in a wide range of weights and varying sizes of mesh. It is usually used as a supporting fabric. Use it to make petticoats, tutus, frills and as a trimming.

Noil: Often confused with raw silk, noil is woven from the short fibres left over after silk has been combed prior to spinning. Unlike most silks, there's very little sheen to a noil cloth and it has a rough surface texture. Try using it for casual shirts, blouses and dresses.

Organdie: Similar to organza, this is a crisp, sheer cotton fabric that makes fantastic special-occasion wear. It is often used as an interlining for other sheer fabrics. It crushes easily, so can look more crumpled when worn.

Organza: Made from silk, polyester or rayon, this is a crisp, plain-woven fabric with more body than chiffon. Organza often has a sheen and is perfect for making sheer overlayers and evening wear.

Oxford cloth: Commonly used for shirt making, Oxford cloth can be either a twill-weave or a plain-weave cotton fabric. It is a strong fabric due to the way two threads are used in the warp.

Pique: A textured cotton that has raised 'cords' running along its length, pique is available in different weights and textures, such as waffle or birds-eye. The lighter weights suit tops, shirts or summer dresses, while heavier weights make great trousers (pants) and structured dresses.

Poplin: A fine weave with a subtle rib running across its width. It is often cotton, but can be made up from wool or silk, too. The weaving process makes it a very strong fabric. Use lightweight varieties for shirts or blouses and heavier weights for trousers (pants).

Rib knit: Knitted with alternate rows of knit and purl stitches, this fabric is characterized by prominent lengthwise ribs, or 'wales', that allow a great deal of stretch across the width of the fabric, making it a great choice for waistbands, cuffs and necklines.

Sateen: Woven with a satin weave, sateen has a light sheen and looks more lustrous than other types of cotton. It is often a blended fabric, available in amazing prints. Heaver than many cottons, it can be used for trousers (pants), jackets and full skirts or dresses.

Satin brocade: This fabric is woven on a jacquard loom to create a floral design on the satin side and is traditionally used for Chinese cheongsam dresses. Use it to make structured dresses, jackets and coats.

Shot taffeta: Woven with two or more coloured yarns, this taffeta has an iridescent quality. It's a great choice for large, full-skirted gowns or costumes.

Spandex and Lycra: Both spandex and Lycra are actually fibres rather than a fabric type. Spandex is elastane fibre, and Lycra is a trade name for a brand of spandex. The fabric commonly described as Lycra or spandex is actually a power knit. This type of knit has exceptional stretch properties due to the addition of the elastane and the four-way stretch. It's commonly used for swimsuits, leotards, cycling clothes and sportswear.

Sweatshirt knit: This fabric has a plain or jersey knit on one side and a brushed, loopy, reverse side. It's the napped, brushed reverse side that makes this knit so distinctive and comfortable to wear. It is a stable knit with limited stretch. Use it to make sweatshirts, hoodies and casual trousers (pants).

Tulle: Finer than net, this is a soft mesh fabric. Available in many fibres, including silk, tulle is the traditional choice for tutus and is often used in bridal wear.

Tussah silk: Also known as wild silk or raw silk, this family of silks has a distinctive coarse, barky texture. Wild tussah worms eat a different diet, making the cloth rougher and less lustrous than other silks. Make it into casual shirts, blouses and dresses.

Tweed: Tweeds are textured woollen cloths that usually have slubs or surface irregularities. They are often woven with different qualities of yarn, including bouclé yarn, which adds to the three-dimensional textured quality of this fabric. Tweeds are suitable for lots of projects, including jackets, dresses, skirts and coats.

Two-way stretch: This term describes any knit fabric that stretches across either the width or the length. Usually the stretch runs from selvedge to selvedge, although it can also run along the length of the fabric only. Two-way stretch is available in various weights and fibres..

Voile: A lightweight, semi-sheer fabric that is similar to lawn but less stiff. It drapes beautifully and can be made from cotton, silk or synthetic fibres. It's a good choice for lingerie, blouses and children's clothes.

CHAPTER 3

Making clothes that fit

The beauty of sewing your own clothes is that you can make garments that fit you properly, instead of having to try to fit into standardized 'off-the-peg' sizes. This chapter sets out everything you need to know to make pattern adjustments to fit your own body shape and size.

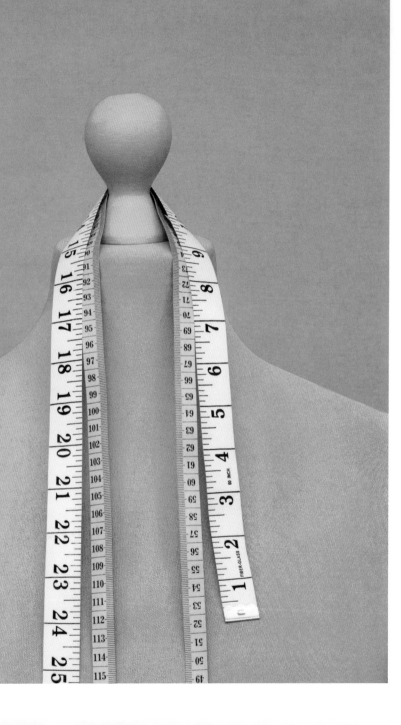

MEASURING AND SIZING

Very few of us have figures that match up with the so-called 'norm': you might, for example, have wide hips or a large or small bust, or your arms or legs might be longer or shorter than average. So the first stage in making clothes that fit well is to find out what your actual measurements are. Don't rely on the size you normally buy in ready-to-wear clothes, as this can vary from one brand to another. Instead, before you buy your paper pattern, take accurate measurements and make a note of them in the chart on page 42. Check your measurements regularly – say, every six months or so.

HOW TO TAKE ACCURATE MEASUREMENTS

Ideally, get someone to help you – they'll be able to make sure the tape is level all the way around your body and doesn't dip at the back, which would distort the measurements. Wear your normal underwear when you're being measured, as that's what you will be wearing underneath any clothing you make; don't measure yourself over your clothes. Stand barefoot – and be sure not to slouch! Hold the tape measure snugly but not tight, then take the following measurements:

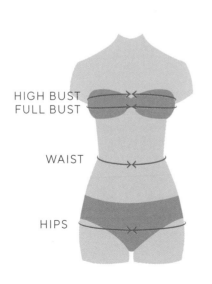

HIGH BUST
FULL BUST

WAIST

HIPS

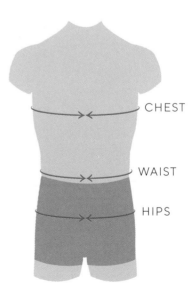

CHEST

WAIST

HIPS

HEIGHT

Standing against a wall, without wearing shoes, measure from the top of your head to the floor.

FULL BUST/CHEST

Measure across the fullest part of your bust, usually at nipple height. For men, make sure the tape measure lies just underneath the armpit to get the widest part of the chest.

HIGH BUST

For women, the high bust measurement is just as important as the full bust measurement, as the difference between the two establishes your bra cup size and indicates whether you will need to make a full or a small bust adjustment (see page 48).Wrap a tape measure above your bust line, high under your armpits.

WAIST

This is the part of your torso just underneath your lowest rib. If you bend to the side, your waist is where your skin creases under your ribs.

HIPS

Your hips are the widest part of your bum and upper thighs. Measure with your feet together. The measurement around your hip bones is called high hip.

INSIDE LEG

Measure the inside of your leg by holding a tape measure as high up on your inner thigh as you can and ask someone to check the length where the tape measure hits the floor. Make sure you stand up straight or else the measurement will come up short.

NAPE (BACK NECK) TO WAIST

Have someone measure you along your spine from your top vertebra to your waist. We all have different-length torsos and if you have a very long or a very short torso, you will probably have to adapt your pattern to suit.

Depending on what type of garment you're making, the following measurements may also be useful:

SLEEVE LENGTH

Slightly bend your elbow and measure from your shoulder to your wrist.

CUFF

Measure the circumference of your wrist. This is useful for making changes to sleeve hems and cuffs.

NECK

Measure all the way around your neck, above the collar bone. This is useful if you're making a garment with a collar or a polo neck.

BICEPS

Measure around the widest part of your biceps. You may need to add extra here if you're making a garment with very tight-fitting sleeves.

MEASUREMENT CHART

Photocopy this chart, then fill in your own measurements (or those of the person you're making the garment for) and take it with you when you go to buy a pattern. This will enable you to see whether or not you need to alter the pattern.

REMEMBER

You're looking at the body size chart on the pattern, not the finished garment size chart.

	MY MEASUREMENTS	THE BODY SIZE MEASUREMENTS ON THE PATTERN	DIFFERENCE
Full bust (or chest for men)			
High bust (for women)			
Waist			
Hips			
Inside leg			
Nape (back neck) to waist			

BUYING THE RIGHT PATTERN SIZE

Home sewing patterns are usually drafted for women who are about 1.65–1.70 m (5ft 5 in.–5 ft 7 in.) tall with a B cup bust, while men's patterns are generally based on a height of 1.73–1.80 m (5 ft 8 in.–5 ft 11 in.). This is designed as a starting point from which makers can adapt their patterns to fit, as that particular height and/or cup size is only applicable to a small proportion of the population (as with all standardized or generic measurements). Compare your measurements from the chart you filled in on page 42 with those on the pattern envelope and choose the pattern size that corresponds to the area of the garment where the best fit is required.

IF YOU'RE MAKING A DRESS, TOP OR JACKET

Select a pattern size based on your bust or chest measurement. Commercial patterns for women tend to be designed for a B cup, which is a difference of no more than 5 cm (2 in.) between the full and high bust measurements. If there's a difference of more than 6.5 cm (2½ in.) between the two, select your pattern size by the high bust measurement. You will then need to alter the pattern to fit the fuller bust, but it should fit better across the shoulders, chest and torso. For pattern alteration tips, see pages 44–55.

IF YOU'RE MAKING A SKIRT OR TROUSERS (PANTS)

Select a pattern size based on your waist measurement unless your hips are two sizes or more larger than your waist; if that's the case, then use your hip measurement and adjust the waist.

It's important to remember that your size may well vary from one brand of pattern to another. You've probably already discovered this when buying ready-to-wear clothes – you might be a size 12 in one shop's clothing and a size 14 in another, for example. This is because every pattern and fashion company has its own size chart: there is no universal size chart based on real people's actual body measurements.

WHAT IF I'M BETWEEN SIZES?

For a closer fit or if you are small boned, select the smaller size. For a looser fit or if you are big boned, select the larger size.

WHAT IF MY HIPS ARE ONE SIZE ON THE PATTERN, BUT MY WAIST OR BUST IS ANOTHER?

Most patterns are multi-sized, which makes it relatively easy to switch from one size of cutting line to another and back again. This is known as 'grading' and you can find out how to do this on page 87.

ALTERING PATTERNS

GRADING IN BETWEEN SIZES

The beauty of having several pattern sizes on the same pattern sheet is that you can easily grade in between the different sizes to suit your measurements. If you are a size 16 on the bust and waist but a size 18 on the hips, for example, you can draw in a smooth line from 16 to 18 in between the waist and the hip to achieve a pattern that's fitted to your personal measurements. You can use a pattern master or a French curve for this to get a really smooth line. It's a great idea to draw this line in a colour, so that you can see where to cut when you have finished grading.

Another way to easily add a bit more space into a pattern is to add to the centre back if you have a seam there. The centre back seam is a straight line, so this way you can easily add up to 2.5 cm (1 in.) without having to redraw the side seams, which will typically have some shaping to them.

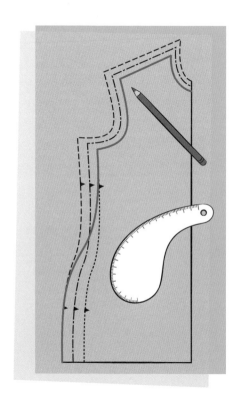

This illustration shows part of the pattern piece for the back of a fitted dress in three sizes – 10, 12 and 14; the black lines are the pattern lines for each size. Let's say your hip measurement is close to size 14, but you're a size 10 at the bust. Trace the fullest size (14) from the hipline down. Using a French curve, draw a new shaped line from the hips to the bust; this is the red line. Your traced pattern is now graded to suit your unique body measurements.

FITTING GUIDELINES

Before you take a look at specific pattern alterations, take the time to read through these general notes.

- To alter your patterns, you will need pattern paper that's sturdy enough to draw on and transparent enough for you to be able to see the original pattern underneath. Tissue paper creases and tears easily, so it's not ideal to use for alterations, though you can transfer your altered patterns to it and use it to cut out your fabric pieces if you wish.

- You will also need adhesive tape to stick your altered pieces back in position (masking tape is good, as you can draw over it), and fine-tipped marker pens to redraw (or 'true') the outlines.

- A long ruler is essential for re-drawing straight lines such as side or centre back seams and a French curve is useful for re-drawing curved lines such as armholes.

- Nearly all garments have some 'ease' built into the pattern so that there is room to move, sit and walk. The amount of ease depends on the type of garment: more ease is included in coats and jackets than in blouses and dresses. To find out how much ease has been incorporated into a garment, compare the Finished Garment Measurements chart with the Body Measurements chart (both of these will be included in commercial patterns). For example, if the Body Measurements chart has a UK size 12 (US size 8) bust measurement of 91 cm (36 in.) and the Finished Garment Measurements chart gives the bust measurement as 106 cm (41¾ in.), that's 15 cm (5¾ in.) ease. When you make pattern alterations, make sure you keep the same amount of ease as in the original pattern.

- First, trace your original pattern pieces onto a separate piece of pattern paper; this way you can draw on and cut into the copy and keep the original pattern intact in case your measurements change in the future or you want to make the garment for someone else. As well as copying the outline, copy any markings such as notches that show where to line one piece up with another, darts, pocket and buttonhole positions, and any text on the pattern. Remember to write the name of the piece (front, back, front facing and so on) on the pattern, so that you know what piece you're working with.

- Start with the largest alterations – first the length, and then any alterations that affect the width (bust, waist, hips).

- If your pattern piece is symmetrical (for example, a skirt front or back piece), you'll need to divide all width alterations by either two or four, because you'll be using the pattern piece(s) to cut a double layer of fabric. For example, if you want to add 2 cm (¾ in.) to the waist of a skirt, you need to add 5 mm (³⁄₁₆ in.) to the front and the same amount to the back; if you added 1 cm (⅜ in.) to each, that would be doubled when you cut the pieces out so you'd have made a 4-cm (1½-in.) adjustment in total.

- Remember to alter any facings or lining pieces by the same amount, so that all the pieces will fit together properly.

- Check whether the alterations have affected the placement of things like pockets or buttonholes. If you've shortened a bodice, for example, you'll need to reposition the buttonholes so that they're evenly spaced.

ALTERING THE LENGTH

Sometimes you need alter the length of a pattern – for example, because your upper body is tall or short or because you have long or short legs. You can determine whether you need more or less length in a bodice by taking your nape-to-waist measurement and comparing that to the pattern. Some patterns have a line (or two parallel lines) that indicates where you can shorten and lengthen, which is positioned in such a way that it doesn't interfere with things like darts. If you don't see such a line on your pattern, you can always add or remove length at the bottom of a pattern if it's a question of a longer or shorter hem, or draw a horizontal line across the pattern. If you are lengthening or shortening by more than 2.5 cm (1 in.), it's best to do it in two different places so as not to alter the shape and proportions of the pattern too much.

LENGTHENING

Cut your pattern across the lengthen/shorten line and spread the pattern pieces apart by the amount that you need. If you are adding length in two different places and you want to add 5 cm (2 in.) in total, spread by 2.5 cm (1 in.) in each area. Slide a piece of paper behind and stick your new pattern down with tape. Then use a ruler or a French curve to smooth out the outlines of your new pattern. This is known as 'trueing'.

SHORTENING

Fold the pattern across the lengthen/shorten line or draw a horizontal line across the pattern. Then make a tuck that's half the amount you want to shorten by: if you want to shorten by 3 cm (1¼ in.), for example, make a 1.5-cm (⅝-in.) tuck. Use tape to stick down the tucks and redraw any outside lines that need to be smoothed out.

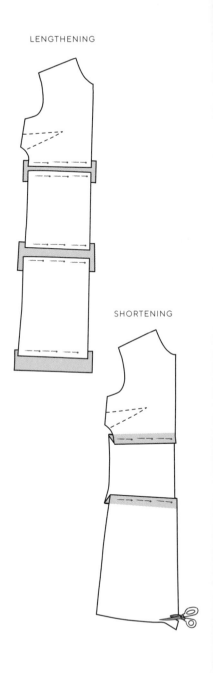

LENGTHENING

SHORTENING

MOVING BUST DARTS UP OR DOWN

Your bust point (the fullest part of the bust) may not be at the same height as the one on your pattern, so you may need to raise or lower the bust darts. You may also need to do this when making a full or small bust adjustment. Measure from your shoulder down to your bust point and compare that measurement with the pattern.

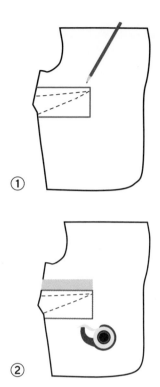

1 Use a ruler and a pencil to draw a rectangular box around the dart. Cut around the box. Slide the box up or down by the amount you need to raise or lower. Make sure you keep the cut edges parallel.

2 Stick the box into its new position and fill in the space with some tracing paper. Use a ruler and pencil to match up and re-draw the outside lines.

ALTERING WAIST DARTS

An easy way to adapt patterns that have waist darts is to make in the darts wider or narrower than the pattern. This is suitable for small pattern alterations to the waist. Divide the alteration between the number of darts – so if you want to take in the waist by 2 cm (¾ in.) and you have four darts, make each dart 5 mm (³⁄₁₆ in.) more than the pattern. The same goes for adding space to the waist: reduce the darts slightly to make the waist a bit bigger.

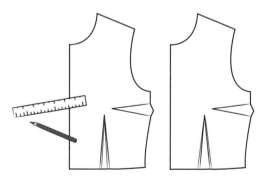

FULL OR SMALL BUST ADJUSTMENTS

Most commercial patterns are cut to fit a B cup, which means some of us will have to adapt our patterns to fit our bust measurements. This sounds more daunting than it actually is and it will make a big difference to how your clothes fit.

If your full bust measurement is bigger than your high bust measurement by more than 6.5 cm (2½ in.), the chances are that your clothes won't fit around your neck, chest and armhole; you'll need to do a full bust adjustment (FBA). If this is the case, use your high bust measurement as your pattern size. If the difference between your high and full bust is much smaller than 6.5 cm (2½ in.), you may have excess fabric around the bust; you'll need to do a small bust adjustment (SBA).

The process for doing a full or a small bust adjustment is the same, except that you are adding space by spreading the pattern for an FBA and reducing space by overlapping the pattern for an SBA.

First, subtract your high bust measurement from your full bust measurement and divide the difference in two. There are two examples below, plus space for you to write down your own measurements.

TIP

Think about the kind of garment you're making before you adjust your pattern. These adjustments are great for garments with fitted bodices, but if you're making a floaty garment with lots of ease then you may be able to get away without making any bust adjustment.

	EXAMPLE 1: FBA	EXAMPLE 1: SBA	MY MEASUREMENTS
Full bust measurement	97 cm (38 in.)	89 cm (35 in.)	
High bust measurement	89 cm (35 in.)	86.5 cm (34 in.)	
Difference	8 cm (3 in.)	2.5 cm (1 in.)	
FBA = half the difference	4 cm (1½ in.)		
SBA = half the difference		1.25 cm (½ in.)	

FULL BUST ADJUSTMENT

1   Hold the pattern paper against yourself, matching the shoulder seamline to the top of your shoulder. Check the bust point; if necessary, move the dart (see page 47).

2   Using a ruler and pencil, draw a straight line from the bust point on the pattern to the hem (make it parallel to the grainline to make sure it's straight). Draw another line from the bust point mark towards the armhole, hitting the lower third of the armhole, or the armhole notch if there is one. This is Line 1. Draw a final line horizontally through the bust dart, meeting Line 1 at the marked bust point. This is Line 2.

3   Cut along Line 1 from the hem to the armhole, leaving it attached by a small hinge at the armhole so that you can pivot the pattern. Cut along Line 2 as well, leaving a small hinge at the tip of the dart.

4   Line up the cut edges of Line 1 so that they have been spread by the amount you need for your FBA. The vertical edges should be parallel to each other, and you will notice that the dart automatically spreads as you do this. The hem is now no longer a nice straight line, so we need to adjust that. Draw a horizontal line parallel to the hem edge, cut along it and move this small piece down until the hem edges are even. Slide some paper behind your new pattern and stick your pattern down with tape.

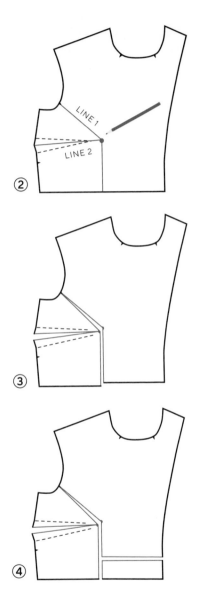

TIP

If your bodice pattern is sewn onto another pattern piece, such as a skirt, make sure you alter that piece too, to compensate for the fact that your bodice pattern is now slightly wider.

SMALL BUST ADJUSTMENT

1   This is the same process as an FBA, but in reverse – you overlap the pieces instead of spreading them apart. Draw in Lines 1 and 2, as for an FBA, and cut along them.

2   Pivot the darted side of the pattern over the other side by the desired amount. The lower edges of the hem will no longer meet, as the side that is being adjusted is shorter.

3   Draw a horizontal line parallel to the hem edge, as for an FBA, cut along it and move this small piece until the hem edges are even.

ADJUSTING PATTERNS WITHOUT DARTS

If your pattern does not have a bust dart, you can create one to make the FBA. Measure 15 cm (6 in.) up from the waist along the side edge and mark with a dot. Draw a straight line from this mark to the bust point on your pattern. Draw a straight line from the lower third of the armhole to the bust point and then straight down to the hemline, as before. Slash and spread the pattern paper by the required amount, add extra pattern paper and tape in place. To close up the side opening that you have just created, draw a dart equal to the width of the side opening, with the top of the dart 2.5 cm (1 in.) from the bust point. Level the hem, as described above.

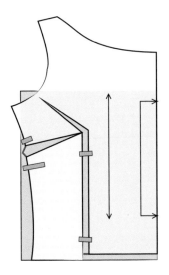

NARROW OR BROAD BACK ADJUSTMENT

If you find that clothes strain at the back and you end up buying a bigger size that then doesn't fit your front, then the chances are you have a broad back. If clothes stand away from your spine along the centre of your back, then a narrow back adjustment can help. This technique is really similar to moving darts. With both these adjustments, remember to alter the front shoulder to match.

NARROW BACK

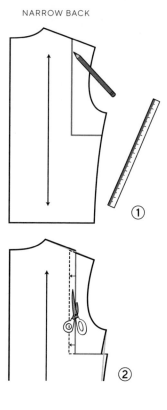

NARROW BACK

1   Some patterns come with an adjustment line for narrow or broad backs drawn on. If your pattern doesn't, draw a vertical line down from the shoulder, starting 3 cm (1¼ in.) from the armhole and ending just below the bottom of the armhole. Draw a second line out to the side of the pattern, at a right angle from this point.

2   Cut along the two lines and slide the armhole side over. Stick the cut-out section in place. Generally a 5-mm (¼-in.) adjustment is enough. Play around with this amount as you develop your fitting skills.

3   Match up and re-draw the side seam. You will also need to shorten the front shoulder a little to match.

BROAD BACK

BROAD BACK

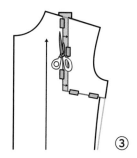

1   As for a narrow back adjustment, draw the two lines and cut out the armhole section of the pattern.

2   Spread the cut pattern pieces apart. You will find that a 6–12-mm (¼–½-in.) adjustment is usually enough.

3   Tape paper in the space and stick the pieces together. Match up and re-draw the outside of the side seam. Lengthen the front shoulder a little to match.

FITTING TROUSERS (PANTS)

There are two common adjustments you can easily make to trouser (pants) patterns: the crotch depth and the crotch length.

ADJUSTING CROTCH DEPTH

Crotch depth is the measurement between your waist and crotch line. You can measure this by sitting on a chair and measuring from your natural waist to the surface of the chair. This measurement is what determines the rise in a pair of trousers and is very different on each person.

To shorten or lengthen the crotch depth on your pattern, use the process described on page 46 for shortening and lengthening in general. Cut along the hip line on your trouser pattern, then spread and add in extra paper to lengthen or make a tuck to shorten. Make sure you true any pattern edges before proceeding.

If no hipline is marked on your pattern, draw a horizontal line by estimating: your hipline lies 18–23 cm (7–9 in.) below your natural waist and use that as your lengthening or shortening line.

ADJUSTING CROTCH LENGTH

Crotch length is the measurement taken from the front waist, through your legs, to your back waist. This measurement differs widely from one person to another and has a lot to do with your body shape.

ADJUSTING CROTCH DEPTH

ADJUSTING CROTCH LENGTH

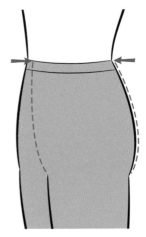

1 Measure yourself, then measure the crotch curve on the pattern. Divide the difference in half; this is the measurement you will use to spread or reduce the curve by.

2 Mark a horizontal line 8 cm (3 in.) below the trouser waist on both your front and back trouser patterns. Cut along this line and leave a hinge at the side seams.

To increase crotch length

Spread the pattern by the amount you calculated in step 1, leaving the side seam as it is. Slide some paper behind and stick your new pattern down with tape. Smooth out the crotch curve.

To reduce crotch length

Overlap the pattern by the amount that you calculated in step 1, leaving the side seam as it is. Tape it in place and carefully smooth out the crotch curve.

....

TIP

If you have a round bum, you might need extra space in the back crotch only. Use this technique to spread the crotch curve on your back trouser pattern only. The same goes for a flatter bum: reduce the crotch curve on the back trouser pattern only.

....

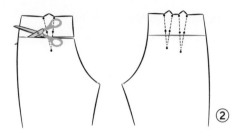

②

TO INCREASE CROTCH LENGTH

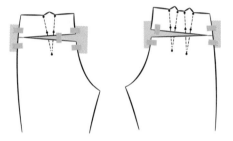

TO REDUCE CROTCH LENGTH

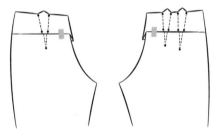

SLASH AND SPREAD

A great way to alter a pattern is to use a technique called 'slash and spread'. With this easy method you can turn a fitted shape into a flared shape: a straight sleeve can become a bell sleeve, an A-line skirt can turn into a more flared skirt, a straight trouser (pants) leg can turn into a flared leg.

Here it's shown on a sleeve pattern – but feel free to experiment!

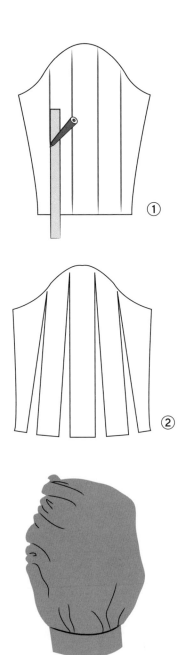

1   Draw vertical lines across your sleeve pattern and cut along these lines, leaving a hinge at the sleeve head. If you draw all the way up to the sleeve head you will get a sleeve that is flared all the way from the top of the sleeve. If you would like a bishop sleeve, you can draw a horizontal line first where you want the volume to start, and then draw vertical lines up to meet this line.

2   You can now spread the different sections by equal amounts, but leaving the sleeve head the same. This means nothing changes in your armhole.

3   Slide pattern paper behind your new pattern and stick your pattern down with tape. Make sure you smooth out the line of the hem.

The variations to this are pretty much endless. You can gather your new sleeve into a cuff if you like or reverse the process by slashing and spreading into the sleeve head to create a gathered sleeve head, as shown right.

TOILES (MUSLINS)

When you've made your pattern alterations, it can be a good idea to make up a 'toile' (muslin); this is a mock-up in a plain fabric such as calico that's a similar weight to the fabric you're using for the garment, on which you can make any final adjustments to before you cut into your expensive fashion fabric. Toiles are also useful if you're new to a pattern or unfamiliar with a particular technique.

You don't always need to make up the whole garment: if you're making a jacket, for example, you could make a half toile – one half of the front, one half of the back and one sleeve. But think about how the garment will function as a whole: if you're making a dress with a fitted bodice and a full skirt, you might be tempted to only make a toile of the bodice if that's the only place you've made pattern alterations – but the skirt will weigh the bodice down and may affect where the waistline sits.

Don't bother finishing seam allowances, adding linings or sewing buttonholes on your toile (you can just use safety pins). However, do put in sleeves as well as zips (zippers) on very fitted garments, as the fabric will gape if you just use pins. Pin up the hem to get an idea of what the finished length will look like, but don't waste time stitching it in place.

Try on your toile; if any of your pattern alterations haven't given you the fit you're after, mark any adjustments on the toile and then refer to them to alter the pattern again. For a complicated garment that you're going to make in a very expensive fabric, you may even need to make more than one toile; it might seem like a palaver, but it's worth it to get a perfect, personalized fit!

CHAPTER 4

Get set!

Before you can start on your sewing project,
it's important to spend some time preparing
and marking your fabric. This chapter takes you
through that preliminary process step by step.

PRETREATING YOUR FABRIC

When you've picked your fabric for a new project, it's hard to resist the temptation to start sewing straight away, but spending a little time preparing your fabric will pay off in the long run. Here are some useful tips on what to do.

PREWASHING

- If you're using a specialist fabric that's dry-clean only, you can go ahead and cut out your pattern pieces without prewashing.

- Most other fabrics have some amount of shrinkage, with cotton typically having the highest percentage – roughly 3–5% – so always wash the fabric before you start sewing a garment. It's really frustrating if you forget to do so and your newly made garment shrinks after the first wash. Launder the fabric according to the care label, which should be given to you by the retailer when you buy the fabric.

- To test how much a fabric will shrink, measure and cut a square, wash it, press it and then measure how much it's shrunk in size.

- Prewashing also gets rid of any coating that might be on the fabric if the fabric has been dyed or printed. A fabric can feel much stiffer when you buy it than after it has been washed for the first time.

- If you've washed a fabric made from synthetic or mixed fibres and the fibres have shrunk in unequal amounts, try to steam press it back into shape to correct the grain.

- Fabrics made from purely synthetic fibres typically shrink much less than fabrics made from natural fibres. After the initial wash, the fabric should have shrunk to its maximum capacity and it won't shrink again.

- You don't have to wash wool before you start, but you should steam it. Use the steam function on your iron and press down onto the wool. Then lift your iron up and move to the next spot. It's important to lift the iron and not drag it across the fabric as this will pull the fabric off grain: wool is very suitable for manipulation, which is how you can steam in beautiful shapes around the collar on a tailored garment, but it also means you have to be careful not to distort the weave when handling it.

- Also think about pretreating any trims you might apply to your garment. If you are applying a metallic braid onto your garment, steam press the braid to make sure it shrinks before you apply it. If you sew a trim or a braid to a garment and the trim or braid shrinks in the wash, it will wrinkle up the fabric around it – and once this has happened, there's nothing you can do about it.

PRESSING

○ After you've prewashed your fabric, it's a good idea to press it once it's dry before you cut out your pieces – unless you're using a fabric that is specifically non-iron, such as nylon or neoprene. Fabrics such as cotton and linen like a hot iron, whereas silk needs a much cooler setting to avoid wrinkling. Remember that fabrics with synthetic fibres contain plastic and plastic melts when it's exposed to high temperatures; so too can your fabric! Press these materials on a cooler setting than you would cottons.

○ Metallic threads tend to shrink a lot, so be sure to give metallic fabrics a good press before you start.

○ Be careful with fabric that has lace inserts when ironing, as lace can easily melt.

UNDERSTANDING YOUR PATTERN

COMMERCIAL PATTERNS

Commercial patterns consist of far more than just the individual pattern pieces. The front of the envelope shows all the different design options, or 'views': for example, a pattern for a dress might have knee-length or maxi options, or two different collar or neckline styles. The back of the envelope has size charts for both body size and finished garment measurements. It will also tell you how much fabric you need, any notions that are required, and which fabrics are recommended. Inside the envelope you will find tissue paper sheets printed with all the pattern pieces ready for you to cut out. In addition, there will be outline drawings of the different views, a diagram of all the pattern pieces (all of which are numbered), step-by-step sewing instructions, and lay plans (see page 64).

....

NOTIONS

Notions, or haberdashery, are all the other bits and pieces you need to complete a garment – fastenings such as zips (zippers), hooks and eyes, and buttons; any decorative trims and so on.

....

COMPLIMENTARY PATTERNS

Lots of books and magazines include complimentary patterns. They will give you the same information as commercial patterns, though some elements may be printed within the body of the book or magazine rather than on the pattern sheets. The best complimentary patterns are full size. You'll need to trace off the pieces you need, as they're often printed on both sides of a sheet, and you may even need to join pieces together if the individual elements are too big; the different halves will be marked with letters that you need to match up before sticking the pieces together with tape. Unless you're making a very simple-shaped garment, such as a child's pinafore dress, it's best to avoid reduced-size patterns as it's all too easy to make mistakes when you're scaling them up to full size, which means that the pieces may not fit together properly.

PATTERN MARKINGS AND TERMINOLOGY

Patterns are full of useful markings, dots, lines and arrows that are all included to help with the cutting out and construction of the garment. Once you understand what each of the symbols or lines mean, you will quickly learn to read the pattern and will find putting the garment together so much easier.

General information

Each pattern piece includes the pattern number, sizes on that particular piece, what the piece is (e.g. FRONT), and simple cutting directions such as, 'CUT 2 IN FABRIC, CUT 1 IN INTERFACING'.

Grainline arrows

Usually these have arrowheads at one or both ends. These lines are pinned parallel to the selvedge to ensure that the pattern piece is correctly angled and cut out.

Angled grainline

'Place to fold' lines have a right-angled arrowhead at each end indicating that the pattern piece should be put on the fold of fabric.

Cutting lines

The outside lines on the pattern pieces are the cutting lines. Different sizes have different line types such as solid, dotted or dashed, which are also numbered by size. In some areas the lines merge, so it is advisable to go over your size line with a coloured pencil before tracing.

Notches

These are triangular symbols shown on the cutting line extending into the seam allowance. These are used to match up seams, front to back, sleeves to armholes. Cut these notches outwards from the cutting line so the seam allowance remains intact in case it is needed to tweak the fit. You will then use them to match garment pieces.

Lengthen or shorten lines

Two parallel lines indicate where the pattern can be made longer or shorter.

Solid lines within the pattern

These indicate buttonhole positions and may also indicate the location of bust line, waist line and hip line.

Circles

These are used to mark the ends of openings such as zips (zippers), or the end of stitch lines such as gathers. They also mark the placement of details such as darts, tabs, belt loops and pockets.

Circle with a cross through it

This symbol marks the main fitting line on the body, at the bust, waist and hip.

Darts

These are shown as V-shaped broken lines with dots. To sew, match the dots, folding the fabric with right sides together, and stitch along the broken line from widest point to tip.

Parallel lines with circles and an arrow line at the bottom

These indicate positions of tucks and pleats. One line is the fold line, the other the placement line (see page 143). Sometimes these are differentiated by a broken line and a solid line. The arrowhead indicates which direction to take the fold.

THE ALL-IMPORTANT GRAINLINE

Before you pin the pattern pieces to your fabric, you need to find what's known as the 'straight grain'. The 'grain' describes the direction of the threads in a woven fabric such as cotton. There are two grainlines on your fabric: the warp, which is the length (or straight) grain and runs parallel to the selvedges, and the weft, which is the cross grain and is perpendicular to the selvedges. (An easy way to remember which is which is that 'weft' rhymes with 'left' and the cross grain runs from left to right.) The main pattern pieces are usually cut on the straight grain, following the warp threads, because the warp grain is generally stronger and less prone to stretching out of shape. This applies to both woven fabric, such as cotton, and knitted fabric, such as the cotton jersey used for T-shirts. The bias grain is an imaginary line at 45° to both the straight and the cross grains; this direction has the most stretch of all. Binding (see page 148) is cut on the bias if it's to be placed around a curved edge such as a neckline.

When you buy your fabric from the shop, the chances are that the cut edges will be a bit wonky and won't line up with each other. There are several ways to straighten the edges and establish the straight grain.

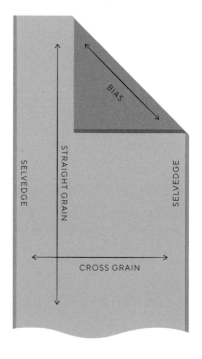

TEARING WOVEN FABRIC

Snip into the fabric a few centimetres (an inch or so) away from one of the cut edges, grasp each side of the snip firmly, and tear across. Pull away any loose threads and this will give you a straight grainline to cut along.

PULLING A THREAD

This method is useful if your fabric will not tear easily. Snip into the fabric close to one cut end, find a weft thread (a thread that goes all the way across the fabric) and start pulling it out. If your fabric puckers up and you can't pull the whole thread out in one go, snip it and then continue pulling for another few centimetres (inches). The space where the thread once was is your straight grainline.

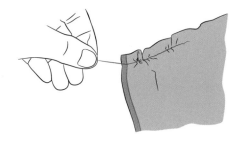

USING A GRIDDED RULER

Lay your fabric out and place one of the grid lines of a quilter's ruler over the selvedge, then draw a line at right angles to the selvedge. If you don't have a quilter's ruler, you can use a set square, or even a right-angled object such as a book, instead.

CHECKING FOR THE STRAIGHT GRAIN

Fold your fabric in half lengthways, lining up the selvedges and the cut edges. If the cut edges don't match, your fabric is still off grain. If it's just slightly off grain then it probably won't affect the pattern too much, so don't spend hours agonizing over it. If it's off by a lot, however, then the seams may twist and stretch because they're being sewn too close to the bias so have another go at straightening the cut edges.

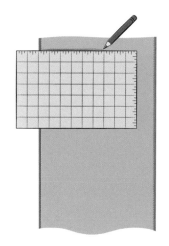

LAY PLANS

Once you've established the straight grain and traced off or cut out the pattern pieces you need, the next stage is to pin the patterns to the fabric and cut them out. Commercial patterns include 'lay plans', which show you how to position the pattern pieces on the fabric in the most economical way. They will also tell you exactly which pattern pieces you need to cut out for the garment you're making (as patterns often include different 'views', you won't necessarily need every single piece in the pattern envelope), and whether or not any pieces need to be cut from lining fabric and/or interfacing. Find the lay plan(s) that relate to the view, size and fabric width that you're using.

The lay plans will also tell you whether or not you need to fold the fabric before you pin the pattern pieces to it. There are various options.

FABRIC FOLDED LENGTHWAYS

For most dressmaking projects the fabric is folded in half along its length, with the selvedges (the finished edges of the fabric) together, so that you cut two perfectly matched pieces from each pattern piece. The fabric is folded with the right sides together, so that any marks can be easily transferred from the pattern to the wrong side of the fabric (see page 68).

FABRIC FOLDED WIDTHWAYS

Sometimes you will need to fold the fabric along its width – if, for example, the fabric would be too narrow for the pattern pieces when folded lengthways, as in this example of a wide circular skirt piece.

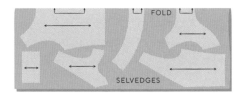

FOLDED LENGTHWAYS

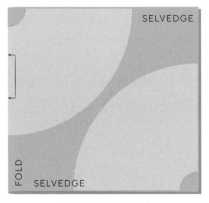

FOLDED WIDTHWAYS

FABRIC CUT IN A SINGLE LAYER

Cutting from a single layer of fabric is useful when you have a patterned fabric where the fabric design needs to match across seams, or to avoid prominent motifs falling awkwardly (see Pattern Matching, page 70). When cutting from a single layer, remember to flip the pattern piece over to cut the second piece in order to get a right- and a left-hand pair.

LAYING THE PAPER PATTERN ALONG THE GRAIN

The grainline is shown on your pattern pieces as a long line with an arrow at each end. It's important that the grainlines are parallel to the selvedges so that the pattern pieces are cut out accurately and will not have unwanted stretch in odd areas.

Place the pattern piece on the fabric, then measure from the selvedge to one end of the grainline and pin that end in position. Then measure the opposite end of the grainline from the selvedge and make sure that this measurement is the same. This ensure that the garment has been cut 'on the grain' so that it won't twist or distort as you wear it. Once the grainline is pinned, you can finish pinning the pattern to the fabric.

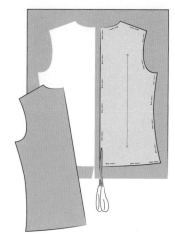

SINGLE LAYER

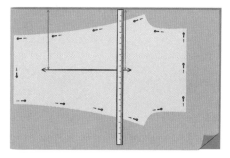

ALONG THE GRAIN

FABRIC WITH A NAP

The term 'nap' refers both to fabrics that have a pile finish, such as velvet, and to fabrics printed with a one-way design – for example, a print of small sprigs of flowers that are all the same way up. When you're laying out fabric with a nap, make sure you position all the main sections of the pattern in the same direction – otherwise light will catch the pile differently and the pattern on one-way designs will be upside down on some pieces. You will also need to allow for buying extra fabric if you're using fabric with a nap. Commercial patterns usually tell you how much extra to buy if you're using a napped fabric and will also have 'with nap' lay plans.

PINNING AND CUTTING

Before you can cut out your fabric and begin sewing, you need to temporarily attach the paper pattern pieces to the fabric – either by pinning them in place or by weighting them down.

PINNING THE PATTERN IN PLACE

If you need to place a piece to the fold, pin the edge that sits on the fold first and then pin out to the corners, spacing the pins about 20 cm (8 in.) apart. Make sure the pins go through both layers of fabric. Keep the pins inside the cutting lines, as they'll damage your scissors if you cut over them.

WEIGHTING DOWN THE PATTERN PIECES

Pins will leave marks in very delicate fabrics, so weights might be a better choice. You can use either purpose-made dressmaking weights or something heavy like paperweights or even stones or cans of beans to hold the paper pattern pieces in position. Some people find it helpful to mark around the outline of the pattern pieces with chalk before they cut. Use dressmaking scissors or a rotary cutter with a special self-healing cutting mat.

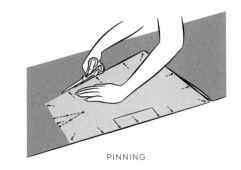

PINNING

WEIGHTING

CUTTING

Place your left hand lightly on the pattern and fabric layers and hold your dressmaker's shears in your right hand (reverse this if you're left-handed). Slide the lower blade under the fabric: the shears should rest on the table top and the fabric should be raised as little as possible. Make smooth cuts, using the full length of the blades where you can; you'll need to use shorter cuts when cutting curves. When you need to move the blades along, move your left hand along too, to hold the fabric steady.

CUTTING AROUND NOTCHES

Notches appear as small triangles on the edges of your pattern pieces and are used to ensure that one pattern piece matches up exactly with another; you need to cut around them when you're cutting out your fabric pieces. They can shown as single, double or even triple triangles, but always cut them as a single unit. Sometimes, you'll even see two sets of notches on the same pattern piece – for example, you might have one notch on the front of a sleeve and two on the back, which you'll need to match to notches on the armhole to ensure that you don't put the sleeve in back to front. Use the tips of your scissors to cut the notches outwards. If you miss one, you can mark the notches by snipping into the seam allowance a little – but don't make the cut too large, or you'll cut into your seam allowance.

TIPS

- Make sure your fabric is completely flat and wrinkle free when you cut out the pieces; avoid leaning heavily on the fabric.

- If you haven't got a large enough table to cut on, place the fabric on the floor.

- Before you start to cut out, double-check the lay plan(s) to make sure you have all the pieces you need and that they're positioned correctly. If you find you've missed out a piece once you've cut, you may not have enough fabric left.

- Iron your paper pattern pieces so that they lie flat on the fabric.

- Check that the fold lines on the patterns are placed exactly on the fold in the fabric – otherwise the pieces will be slightly too big when they're cut out.

- Don't lift up the shears or the fabric while you're cutting, as the fabric will shift out of position.

- Don't cut through any fold lines!

TRANSFERRING PATTERN MARKINGS

Some pattern markings have to be transferred to your fabric pieces before you remove the paper patterns, as they show where one piece needs to be matched up with another or where to position features such as pockets, darts and zips (zippers).

TRACING WHEEL AND DRESSMAKER'S CARBON PAPER

Select a colour of carbon paper that will show up on your fabric and position it with the coloured (carbon) side of the paper facing the wrong side of the fabric. Run the tracing wheel around the pattern to produce a line of coloured dots on the wrong side of the fabric.

To mark two identical pieces at once or a piece that's cut on the fold and has symmetrical markings such as darts on both sides, fold your carbon paper in half so that you have the coloured side on both sides, then slot it in between the two layers of fabric. Use your tracing wheel as per usual and mark two lines at the same time.

TAILOR'S CHALK AND AIR- OR WATER-SOLUBLE MARKERS

These can all be used to add seam allowances, draw in hemlines, mark the position of darts or other features, and mark anywhere where you need to see a stitching line. Always test them on a scrap of your chosen fabric to make sure the lines will brush out or disappear after a wash.

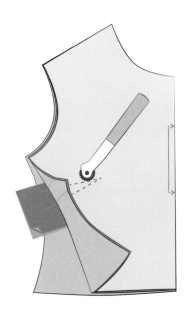

PIN MARKING

This is a super-useful technique for marking dots and circles on cottons and robust fabrics.

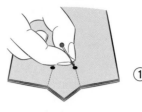

1 Pass a pin through the centre of the circle of the mark you want to transfer. Slide the pin all the way through the pattern and both layers of fabric.

2 Open the two layers of fabric without removing the pin.

3 Use a chalk slab or a marking pencil to mark where the pin pricks the fabric. Do the same on the other side of the fabric

MARKING WITH TAILOR'S TACKS

If you are sewing delicate fabrics, sheers or woollen fabrics on which the chalk/pen marks won't show, mark positions with thread markings called tailor's tacks.

TAILOR'S TACKS

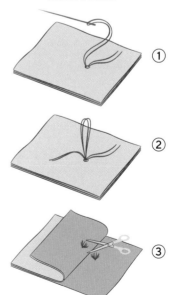

1 Thread a needle with double thread and make a stitch through the circle, through the pattern and both layers of the fabric, leaving at least 2.5 cm (1 in.) thread tail.

2 Make a second stitch at the same spot, leaving a long loop in the stitch. Cut the thread with a long thread tail.

3 Snip into the loop, then gently pull the fabric layers apart and snip the threads in the middle so that some thread is on either side of your pieces.

PATTERN MATCHING

Pattern matching means ensuring that a fabric print runs continuously across seams. If you have a very big print, you can also think about the positioning of the print on your garment: if you have a big floral design on a plain background, for example, it would be a shame to end up with a garment where the flower is slightly off centre or is cut off by a side seam.

Some patterns are random, and however hard you try, you will never be able to match these. Others will have a 'repeat', which is the length across or down the fabric before the pattern repeats itself. The easiest way to understand this is with stripes. For example, if you have a fabric with alternating blue and white horizontal stripes, the repeat will be the measurement from the beginning of the blue stripe to the end of the white one. Some fabrics repeat both vertically and horizontally – for example, checks. Floral and other designs work in exactly the same way, although the repeat is not necessarily so obvious. When you buy fabrics, you will find they are labelled with the length of the repeat. The bigger the repeat, the more fabric you will need to allow for matching, as you will need to space your pattern pieces out to capture a certain part of the print.

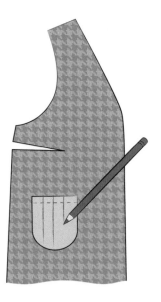

PATTERN MATCHING A SMALL PIECE

If you need to pattern match a small piece, such as a pocket on a coat, position the paper pattern piece on top of the material where the pocket will sit and draw a small section of the print onto your paper. Remove your paper and pin it onto the fabric that you're cutting the pocket from, matching the print lines, so that the print aligns.

MATCHING BOLD PRINTS

It can be easiest to cut out each piece on a single layer to make sure you get an exact match. With a fabric that's placed on the fold, you won't be able to see what's happening on the reverse.

1 Start by folding the paper pattern piece in half both ways to find the centre. Crease and unfold. Lay the fabric on a flat surface right side up. If you are using a fabric with a large pattern repeat, position the paper pattern over the design, using the creases to help you decide how to position the motifs. Using a very soft pencil, mark the vertical and horizontal positions of the motifs on the tissue paper. Pin the pattern piece in position on the fabric and cut out the first piece.

2 Turn the pattern piece over and reposition it on the right side of the fabric, matching the design motifs with the marks you have made on the pattern piece. Pin in place and cut out the second piece. Repeat in the same way with any other pattern pieces. You can use this method to perfectly match large, bold motifs on all fabrics.

INTERFACING

Interfacing is added to the reverse of some areas in a garment in order to add body and support. Areas that need to be interfaced include buttonholes, waistbands, front facings, collars and cuffs. Apply interfacing to the relevant pieces before you begin making up the garment.

TYPES OF INTERFACING

There are three main categories. **Non-woven** interfacing is made from pressed fibres with a felt-like appearance; there is no grainline to follow so pattern pieces can be laid out in any direction. **Woven** interfacings have a fabric grain and are handled in the same manner as fabrics. They are more flexible than non-woven types. **Knitted** interfacings have two-way stretch in order to move like knitted fabrics, adding support without changing the handle of the garment.

All types can be iron-on (fusible) or sew-in and come in super-light, light, medium or heavyweight. Depending on the type, interfacings may be available in white, charcoal, black or beige.

APPLYING INTERFACINGS

IRON-ON (FUSIBLE) INTERFACING

Iron-on interfacing has a glue applied to one side, which can be seen as a slightly raised surface that may also slightly glisten or shine.

1   Cut the interfacing to the size of the pattern pieces. If you are using medium to heavyweight fabrics, trim the interfacing all the way around so that it fits just within the stitching line.

2   Place the fabric wrong side up on the ironing board with the interfacing glued side down on top. Cover with a damp press cloth.

3   Check the manufacturer's instructions to find out what temperature to set your iron to and whether steam is applicable. Place the iron on top of the press cloth and press down, holding the iron in the same position for 10–15 seconds. Lift the iron, move to an adjacent area and press down again. Repeat until the whole area has been pressed.

4   If the corners of the interfacing can be lifted away, press again until it has completely bonded. Leave the interfaced piece to cool completely before continuing to work with it.

SEW-IN INTERFACING

Sew-in interfacing is sewn to the reverse of the main fabric. It is the best choice where the heat and moisture needed for fusible interfacing would damage the fabric – for example, on pile fabrics such as velvet.

1 Use the appropriate pattern piece(s) to cut out the interfacing.

2 Stitch the interfacing to the reverse of the main fabric piece, just inside the seam allowance.

3 To reduce bulk in the seams, trim away excess interfacing close to the stitching, cutting the corners off at an angle.

USING INTERFACING

° Iron-on interfacings are quick to apply, but it is very important to fuse them completely and permanently to avoid them 'bubbling' under the fabric when laundered at a later date.

° Choose an interfacing that is lighter than the fabric to which it's being applied.

° Apply sew-in interfacings to the garment, not the facings, to avoid the seam allowances showing through and help prevent facings from rolling out.

° With iron-on interfacing, the time required to achieve a good bond varies depending on the interfacing and fabric weight. Always test on a sample first.

° On very lightweight, transparent fabrics, use an extra layer of the main fabric instead of interfacing to avoid spoiling the transparency of the fabric.

CHAPTER 5

Sew simple!

This chapter sets out everything you need to know to create stylish, well-fitting garments for all the family. Packed with clear step-by-step illustrations and useful tips, it's your go-to resource for successful sewing.

THREADING YOUR SEWING MACHINE

FILLING UP THE BOBBIN

All sewing machines do this in a similar way, but consult your manual for specific details.

1 Drop an empty bobbin onto the bobbin winder pin and pop your reel of thread onto the spool pin.

2 Pass the thread into the middle of the bobbin tension guide – it's important to get right in between these discs so that your thread stays taut.

3 Pass the thread over to the bobbin and then manually wind it around the middle a few times from left to right, starting with the thread at the back. This helps the thread to 'grip' when you start winding on by machine.

4 Click the bobbin winder pin from left to right to engage the winder.

5 Push your foot on the foot control pedal and watch the thread begin to wind on. The thread should look taut; if it looks saggy, then check that it's right in between the bobbin tension discs.

6 Once the bobbin is full, stop pressing the foot control pedal and click the bobbin winder pin back over to the right.

7 Snip the thread, then drop the filled bobbin into its case, either on top of the machine bed or into the removable case at the front of the machine.

TIP

Always use bobbins intended for your make and model of machine; although they may look the same, sometimes they are very slightly different in size and thus fit.

THREADING UP THE TOP OF THE MACHINE

Most machines have numbered guidelines marked on the machine to help you.

1 Pass the thread behind the first thread guide, then slide it downwards through the slit in the machine. Sometimes you can see a pair of numbered discs here; this is another tension guide to keep your thread taut.

2 Guide the thread under and upwards from the next thread guide. You may need to turn the needle wheel until you see a silver lever (the take-up lever) rise above the top of the machine. Pass the thread from right to left around the take-up lever.

3 Pass the thread back down through the second vertical slit.

4 At the very top of the needle there is a hook; make sure your thread sits around this hook, which will hold the thread flat before it reaches the eye of the needle.

5 Thread the needle by passing the end of the thread through the eye from the front towards the back. Lots of modern machines have attached needle threaders, which can help if you find this bit fiddly.

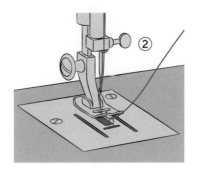

PULLING UP THE BOBBIN THREAD

This is the bit most beginners find the trickiest. It's worth practising a few times until you get the process set in your mind. Again, refer to your sewing machine manual for detailed instructions.

1 Make sure the sewing or presser foot is in the raised position.

2 Hold onto the thread coming from the needle with your left hand. Turn the needle wheel towards you with your right hand. You'll start to see the top thread 'wrapping' around the lower thread and pulling up through the throat plate.

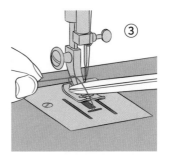

3 Once you see a loop wrapped over the top thread, stop turning the needle wheel. Use your fingers or the point of a small pair of scissors to pull up the loop until it's a single tail.

4 Put the bobbin cover on if it is not already in place. Make sure both threads are sitting in between the sewing foot and the throat plate.

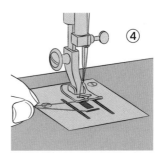

....

TIP

If the thread splits before it goes through the needle, re-snip the end with a sharp pair of scissors and try again. If it's still hard to thread, tap the cut end with your teeth. This 'fans' the end, making it easier to thread.

....

PRACTICE MAKES PERFECT!

You're now ready to sew your first line of machine stitching. Before launching into your first project, practise on scraps of spare fabric to build up your confidence.

MOVING FORWARD IN A STRAIGHT LINE

Sewing forwards in a straight line is used not only to create seams, but also to tack (baste), zigzag to neaten edges and do pretty much all machine sewing.

1 Begin by raising your sewing foot, and passing your fabric under the foot. Bring your needle into the fabric about 1 cm (⅜ in.) from the fabric edge. Lower the sewing foot and lightly hold onto the two threads while you use the foot pedal control to start the machine moving forward... easy!

2 Once you've sewn a couple of stitches, press and hold the reverse button and sew a few stitches backwards. This will fix the stitching and prevent the fabric from tangling or being pulled into the feed dogs at the start.

3 Once you've done a couple of stitches backwards, release the reverse button and continue sewing forwards.

TIP

For 99% of seams, your stitch length should be set at 2–3mm (about ⅛ in.).

TURNING CORNERS

There aren't many sewing projects that can be made using just straight lines, so at some point you will inevitably need to turn a corner on the sewing machine.

1 When you've reached the point at which you need to turn, stop sewing and lower the needle all the way into your fabric, using either the needle or the balance wheel at the side of the machine.

2 Raise the sewing foot and pivot the fabric around until the sewing foot faces the direction in which you wish to continue sewing.

3 Lower the sewing foot and continue sewing forwards again.

TIP

Avoid threads tangling at the start of your stitching by holding both needle and bobbin thread taut in your left hand for at least the first 2.5 cm (1 in.).

STITCH TENSION

All sewing machines have a tension control for the top thread; most have one for the bobbin thread, too. Before you start a project take a small doubled piece of the fabric you are about to sew and the right needle size and thread for the fabric type and weight. Thread your machine with different colours of thread for the top and bobbin threads, so that you can easily differentiate between them. Stitch for about 15 cm (6 in.).

If the thread tension is correct, the stitches look smooth and flat on both sides of the seam and the needle and bobbin threads interlock midway between the two layers of fabric.

If the needle thread tension is too loose, the top thread will show loops on the underside.

If the needle thread tension is too tight, the bobbin thread will be pulled up to the top side.

However, there are other things that can cause the fabric to pucker or seams to look uneven, so run through this checklist before you attempt to alter the tension settings:

- Have you threaded the machine properly? Most tension discs close when the presser foot is down, so always thread the machine with a raised foot.
- Are you using the right size of needle for the fabric? (See page 19.)
- Is the needle bent or damaged?
- Are you using the same weight of thread for both the top and bobbin threads?
- Are the tension disks clean and lint free?
- If you're sure that it's the stitch tension that's the problem, check the instruction

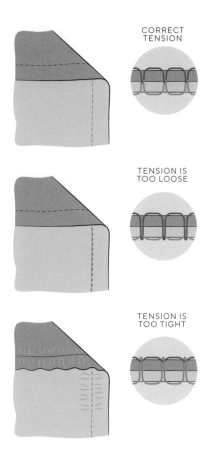

CORRECT TENSION

TENSION IS TOO LOOSE

TENSION IS TOO TIGHT

manual to see how to adjust the top thread tension, then stitch another sample. If it hasn't resolved the issue, you may need to adjust the bobbin thread tension, too; use a small screwdriver to turn the screw clockwise to tighten and anticlockwise to loosen. Be cautious, though – the tiniest of adjustments here will make a big difference.

PINNING

Pinning seams before you sew them really is the best way to get excellent results first time, and avoid having to unpick. There are two ways to pin. In practice, you'll probably find that you use a mixture of the two.

Vertical pinning

In vertical pinning, the pins are parallel to the edge of the seam allowance and the point is facing towards the sewing machine. This type of pinning is really secure and is the best way to pin fiddly things like zips (zippers). It's also a good alternative to tacking (basting).

Horizontal pinning

This is the way many people prefer to pin. The pins are slipped into the fabric layers at a 90° angle to the edge of the seam allowance. The point of the pin faces into the piece, with the head towards the outside. Horizontal pinning is great for pinning seams and the pins are easier to remove as you sew than vertical pins.

VERTICAL PINNING

HORIZONTAL PINNING

HAND AND MACHINE STITCHES

These hand stitches are often used in dressmaking and are all simple to master. Some (such as tacking/basting stitches) are temporary and are removed once a seam has been machine stitched; others are used to permanently secure hems and gaps left in seams when pieces are turned right side out.

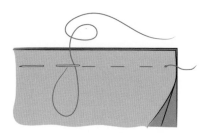

EVEN TACKING

TACKING (BASTING)

These are long hand stitches used to keep layers together temporarily while you machine the seam. They're quick to do and are especially useful if you are using a slippery fabric like silk or satin, or one with a nap such as velvet or corduroy. Use a thread colour that stands out well against the fabric.

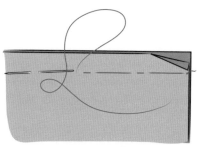

UNEVEN TACKING

Even tacking

Use a needle with thread knotted at one end. Make long running stitches about 1 cm (½ in.) long. In fiddly areas, you might want to make shorter stitches. Finish off with two tiny stitches on top of each other.

Uneven tacking

If you have a long seam (or hem) to tack, make it speedy by alternating long – 7.5-cm (3-in.) – stitches with tiny ones.

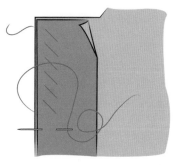

DIAGONAL TACKING

Diagonal tacking

This is used where two pieces of fabric need to be secured in position over a large area, such as linings and interlinings, so that the layers don't creep while you're constructing the garment.

SLIPSTITCH

This stitch is great for sewing double-turned hems on luxury fabrics such as silk.

Anchor your knot inside the fold of the hem. Pick up a small thread of the garment fabric, then pass the needle back into the folded edge of the hem and slide it 1 cm (⅜ in.) along the fold. Repeat the stitches until the hem is complete. All that should be visible is a series of V-shaped stitches on the wrong side and a discreet needle prick on the right side.

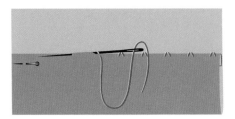

SLIPSTITCH

HERRINGBONE STITCH

Also called a catch stitch, this works really well on thick, bulky fabrics like wool or heavy drill. It's worked from left to right, and is best suited to single-turned hems.

Neaten the raw edge of your hem. Press up the desired hem allowance. Start by anchoring a knot behind the hem allowance. Making a diagonal stitch to the right, catch one thread of fabric from the garment above the hem. Then making a second diagonal stitch catch a deeper thread of fabric from the hem allowance. Repeat this all around the hem. Finish off with a couple of backstitches in one place.

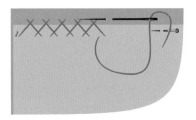

HERRINGBONE STITCH

FELL OR VERTICAL STITCH

This is a variation of slipstitch, and is the best stitch for attaching linings.

Anchor the knot inside the folded edge of the hem or lining. Pick up a tiny stitch in the garment fabric, and pass the needle diagonally back into the fold about 3 mm (⅛ in.) from the edge. Repeat along the hemline. You'll end up with a series of vertical stitches along the folded edge of the lining/hem.

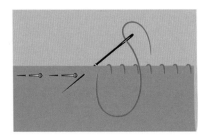

FELL OR VERTICAL STITCH

MACHINE STITCHING TECHNIQUES

There are machine stitching techniques that you'll come across time and time again.

Easing/ease stitch

This is used to gather fabric to ease it into a smaller piece (e.g., when setting in sleeves) or on a curved hem. Increase the stitch length to 4 and sew just inside the seam allowance; on sleeve heads, sew again 3 mm (⅛ in.) from the first row. Pull up the stitching to gather the piece to the required length.

Edge stitching

This is the same as topstitching, but it is sewn much closer to the edge, hence its name.

Gathering

Set the longest stitch length and sew just inside the seam line, leaving a long thread tail.. Pull up the bobbin thread from either end to gather the fabric evenly. To gather by hand, use double thread and take long running stitches, pulling up the fabric as required.

Staystitching

Staystitching is done just inside the seam allowance, to prevent bias-cut or curved areas from stretching out of shape while you work on them. Sew with a regular stitch length just inside the seam allowance.

Topstitching

This is stitching that is visible on the surface. Topstitched hems are usually sewn about 1 cm (⅜ in.) from the edge.

Understitching

This is used to anchor the seam allowance to a facing to prevent the facing from rolling out. Sew the facing to the garment, then press both facing and seam allowances away from

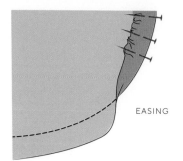

EASING

STAYSTITCHING

TOPSTITCHING

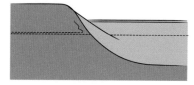

UNDERSTITCHING

the garment. With the facing uppermost, sew close to the seam on the facing, catching the seam allowances underneath as you sew.

SEAMS

The seam is the basic building block of all sewing. There are many types of seams, but these are the ones you need to get started.

STRAIGHT SEAM

Straight seams can be pressed 'open' or 'closed'; your pattern instructions will tell you which one to use.

AN 'OPEN' STRAIGHT SEAM (1)

The seam allowances are pressed open so that they sit on either side of the seam line, creating a flat look from the outside of the garment.

A 'CLOSED' STRAIGHT SEAM (2)

Both sides of the seam allowance are pressed together over to one side. It creates a slightly heavier look from the outside than an open seam, but is more robust.

FLAT FELL SEAM

This seam is useful for reversible items, or to give added strength. Sew with the wrong sides of the fabric together. Press the seam allowances to one side and then trim the under seam allowance to a scant 3 mm (⅛ in.). Fold the edge of the upper seam allowance under by 6 mm (¼ in.), overlapping the under seam allowance. Stitch in place through all layers. Lengthen the stitches for the second row of stitching for the thicker fabric layers.

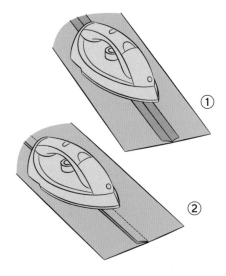

FLAT FELL SEAM

TIP

Dressmaking seam allowances are usually 1.5 cm (⅝ in.). To keep the width consistent, line up the raw edges of the fabric with the relevant guideline on the needle plate of the machine.

FRENCH SEAM

A French seam is great for transparent fabrics or when the inside of a garment may show.

1 First sew the seam with the **wrong** sides of the fabric together, taking a scant 6-mm (¼-in.) seam allowance. Trim the seam allowance to 3 mm (⅛ in.).

2 Re-fold the fabric so that the **right** sides are together and the previous seam is right on the edge. Press. Stitch with a 1-cm (⅜-in.) seam allowance.

CURVED SEAMS

To sew curved seams, follow these simple steps.

1 Stitching within the seam allowance, staystitch any curves such as curved bust seams, necklines and raglan sleeves (see page 83).

2 Pin the two curves together. One curve will be convex (outward) and one curve will be concave (inward). You can only pin convex to concave, and not the other way around. Pin any balance marks or notches first and distribute the pins evenly, pinning at a 90° angle to the seam line. For extreme curves you may have to snip into the seam allowance to manoeuvre around the curves.

3 Reduce your stitch length slightly to 2.5 to achieve a smooth curved line, then stitch your seam from top to bottom.

FRENCH SEAM

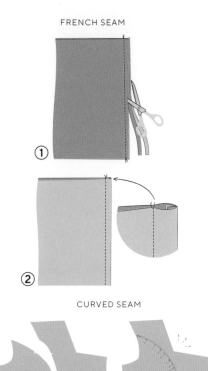

CURVED SEAM

TIPS

° **Stitch all seams in the same direction – e.g. from hem to top.**

° **At the end of a seam take both threads to the back of the work, feed them between the fabric layers within the seam allowance, pull taut and snip off so that they disappear into the seam allowance.**

° **Press all seams (first from the wrong side to embed the stitching and then from the right side) before crossing over them with more stitching.**

SEAM FINISHES

If you leave all the raw edges inside your garments unfinished, they will unravel over time, particularly when laundered – and eventually the seams may fall apart. You need to neaten, or 'finish', the seams to prevent this from happening.

USING A ZIGZAG STITCH ON YOUR SEWING MACHINE

If you have a sewing machine with a zigzag function, this is the easiest and most popular way to neaten the edges of your seam allowance. Set the stitch to the widest available, and play around with the stitch length. Start with a 5-mm (¼-in.) width and a 2-mm (⅛-in.) length. Line up the needle so that it 'zigs' inside the fabric and 'zags' next to the edge.

Zigzagging an open seam (1)

When you have an open seam, zigzag both sides of the seam allowance separately.

Zigzagging a closed seam (2)

For a closed seam, zigzag the two sides together as one layer.

USING AN EDGE STITCH ON THE SEWING MACHINE (3)

This is a great technique if you have a vintage machine without a zigzag function. Use this technique on open seams only, as it's too bulky for a closed seam. Working from the wrong side of the seam allowance, press under a very narrow fold of about 3 mm (⅛ in.) and stitch

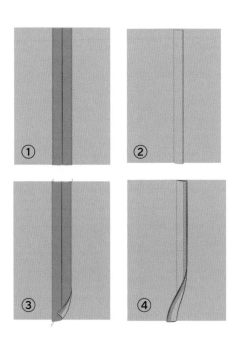

with a line of straight stitches. You can fold as you sew, so there's no need for pins.

NEATENING WITH AN OVERLOCKER/SERGER (4)

An overlocker (serger) is a machine specifically designed to finish the edges and trim in one process, but using a zigzag stitch is just as good for most home sewing. The overlocker has a blade, and if you're new to sewing this can be a little intimidating. An overlocked edge gives a neat, professional finish to your seams.

REDUCING BULK

Once you've sewn a seam, you may be instructed to trim, grade, clip or notch the seam allowances to allow the seam to lie flat or sit smoothly on the right side.

Trimming (1)

This is done when the full width of the seam allowance will look bulky on the right side of the garment. It's often done on enclosed seams like a French seam (see page 85). Use sharp scissors to trim away the excess fabric.

Clipping corners (2)

Where you have stitched around a corner, you need to trim away the bulk before turning it through, otherwise you'll be left with a lumpy, bumpy finish. Trim quite close to the stitching, making sure you don't snip into any stitches. Simply snip off the corner; if it's very pointed, taper the sides well.

Grading (3)

This is done mostly on thick fabric, so that the cut edges inside the seam are staggered. Sometimes only one side of the seam allowance is trimmed away; sometimes both sides are trimmed, but to different depths. It's often done on seams such as flat fell seams.

Notching (4)

On an outwardly curved seam, snip triangular wedges along the area of the seam that has the greatest curve., spacing them evenly. On inward curves, such as around a neckline, cut regularly spaced slits into the seam allowance rather than notches.

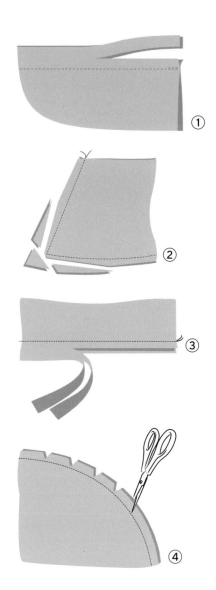

HEMS

Whatever method of hemming you use, first you need to prepare the hem allowance.

PREPARING THE HEM ALLOWANCE

The hem allowance adds weight to the hem and helps it hang nicely. An A-line skirt in lightweight cotton needs only a little hem allowance of 2.5–5 cm (1–2 in.), while medium-weight straight skirts, dresses, jackets and trousers (pants) benefit from a hem allowance of up to 8 cm (3 in.).

1   Preferably hang the garment for 24 hours prior to hemming to allow the fabric to settle and even drop if it is cut on the bias. You can then straighten the hem edge before neatening and hemming.

2   Mark the hem level from floor upwards, placing pins parallel to the hem line.

....

TIP

When marking hem levels, make sure that the person for whom the garment is being made is wearing the appropriate underwear and shoes, as this affects how the garment will hang.

....

3   Working on a flat surface, with the garment turned wrong side out, fold up the hem at the marked hemline,

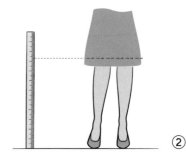

②

④

matching the side, centre back and front seams. Place pins vertically, removing the horizontal pins.

4   Decide on the hem allowance and mark the upper limit. Trim the hem allowance even if necessary.

5   Finish the raw edge of the hem allowance prior to stitching the hem in place by zigzag stitching or overlocking (serging) close to the edge and then trimming close to the stitching. Fabrics that do not fray, such as stretch knits and fleece, do not need to be neatened.

DOUBLE-TURNED HEM

A double-turned hem looks neat and there are no raw edges visible, so it's a strong hemming technique, too.

It can be achieved in two ways. You can either fold up the hem by half the required amount and then again by the same amount, which folds the raw edge under. (However, if your hem is deep, the enclosed edge should be narrower than the hem depth, as this gives a smoother finish.) Alternatively, you can fold up the entire hem allowance and then tuck the raw edge inside.

Press and stitch close to the inner fold of the turned-up hem. Generally you will be working from the wrong side of the garment, so make sure that the bobbin has thread to match the fabric. If desired stitch again, working in the same direction close to the hem edge, to provide two parallel lines of stitching.

DOUBLE-TURNED HEM

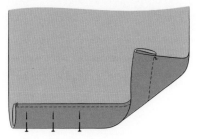

TWIN NEEDLE TOPSTITCHED HEM

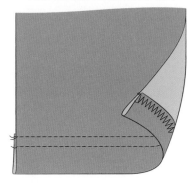

....

TIP

When topstitching, make the hem stitching a feature of the garment by using a contrast thread colour or decorative stitch.

....

TWIN NEEDLE TOPSTITCHED HEM

A twin needle has two needles on one shank. They are available with different width gaps between the needles, ranging from 1.6 mm (1/16 in.) to 6 mm (1/4 in.) and in different weights, such as fine 65/9 up to jeans needles 100/16, as well as universal sharps, ballpoint and stretch varieties.

For hemming, a gap of approx 3–4 mm (about 1/8 in.) is ideal. On the top you will get two perfectly parallel rows of stitching, and on the underside a zigzag-looking stitch; it is therefore essential that you sew from the right side of the garment. The results look like the kind of hems you frequently see on high-street garments.

FULL OR CURVED HEMS

On a very full or curved hem, you will have to ease in some of the excess hem allowance before turning up the hem.

1 First prepare the hem allowance (see page 88).

2 Ease stitch (see page 83) 6 mm (¼ in.) from the raw edge, increasing the stitch length to 4–5. Then gently pull up the stitching (using the bobbin thread) and turn up the hem allowance. The slight ripples and gathers should be in the hem allowance only, leaving the garment edge smooth and ripple free.

3 Turn the raw edge under, tuck inside the hem allowance and topstitch in place.

BLIND HEMMING

A blind hem is not supposed to be visible from the outside, although a machine-stitched blind hem may leave tiny ladder-like stitches. First neaten the raw edge by zigzag stitching or overlocking (serging) close to the edge and trimming close to the stitching. (Non-fray fabrics do not need to be neatened.)

BLIND HEM BY MACHINE

A blind hem stitch is created by a few straight stitches, then one zigzag stitch to the left. Use a blind hem foot, which has a vertical guide in the centre protruding below the foot, against which the hem allowance fold is butted.

1 Pin up the hem allowance and tack (baste) at right angles to the hem edge.

FULL OR CURVED HEMS

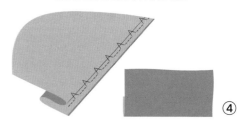

②

BLIND HEMMING BY MACHINE

④

2 Fold the hem allowance back on itself along the line of tacking stitches so that about 1 cm (⅜ in.) of the neatened hem edge extends beyond the fold..

3 Snap on the blind hem foot and butt the hem allowance fold against the vertical guide on the foot.

4 Select the blind hem stitch and test stitch. The straight stitch should be on the hem allowance only and the zigzag just catching in the fold. If it takes too big a stitch into the fold, reduce the stitch width and try again. Once you are happy with the positioning, stitch your hem.

5 Fold the hem back to the wrong side and press carefully to set the stitches, avoiding pressing the hem edge which should be left soft and rounded.

BLIND HEM BY HAND

Use a thread colour to match the garment.

1 Turn up the hem and tack (baste) it in place close to the fold, matching any seams.

2 Starting at a seam, fold back 13 mm (½ in.) of the hem allowance and hold it folded down with one hand. Secure the thread to the seam allowance of the seam, then bring the thread up through the folded-back hem allowance. Take the needle through to the garment and pick up just one or two fibres of the garment fabric before bringing the needle back through the folded hem allowance approximately 6–13 mm (¼–½ in.) in front of the last stitch. Continue along the hem, allowing the folded-back hem allowance to fall back in place as you go.

PIN HEMMING

This method works really well on curved hems and slippery fabrics. Rather than struggle trying to fold two delicate hems on top of one another, it involves stitching the hem twice.

1 Press under a 1-cm (⅜-in.) fold all the way around the bottom of the piece to the wrong side. Work slowly and use a seam-measuring gauge to get an evenly pressed fold.

2 Using a straight stitch on the machine, sew 3 mm (⅛ in.) from the folded edge. Using sharp scissors, trim away the excess fabric close to the stitch line.

3 Press up the narrow hem you've stitched, so that the raw edges are hidden. Stitch a second line, following the first row of stitches, or 3 mm (⅛ in.) from the outside edge. Press the hem flat.

BLIND HEM BY HAND

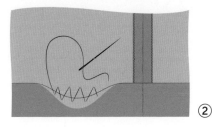

②

PIN HEMMING

②

③

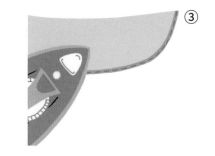

DARTS

Darts help shape garments to fit over body contours at the bust, hips, through the midriff and at the shoulders. Most darts are V-shaped, with the widest part at the outer edge, tapering to a point in the garment. Contour darts, which are widest in the middle and taper to a point at either end, are used on fitted and semi-fitted dresses; the widest part fits into the waistline and then tapers off to fit the bust and hips, or the back and hips.

SINGLE DARTS

1   Mark the dart position and length, then fold the fabric right sides together, so that the marks sit one on top of the other (check by pinning through the layers). Either pin along the stitching line or mark the line with a chalk pencil and then pin at right angles to the dart.

2   Starting at the garment edge, sew towards the point, taking the last two or three stitches in the fold of fabric at the very point. Do not backstitch; instead, leave long thread tails and knot the ends together.

3   Press waist darts towards the centre of the garment and press bust darts downwards.

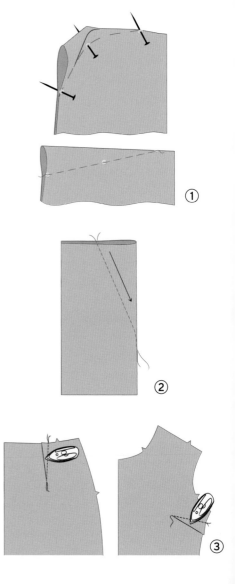

CONTOUR DARTS

A contour dart (also known as a double-ended dart or fisheye dart) can be used to shape the back of the garment from shoulder to hip, or the front from below bust to hip.

1 Fold out the dart, with right sides together, and pin or tack (baste). Start stitching at the centre, stitching to one point, then leave the thread tails to knot.

2 Flip the fabric over to stitch the other side, starting at the centre again and slightly overlapping the stitching at the centre by 1 cm (⅜ in.). Stitch to the other point, stitching the last two or three stitches on the fold.

3 To help the dart curve into the body and the folded fabric to lie flat, cut a wedge out of the widest part of the dart fold. On fabrics that fray easily, add a tiny dab of Fray Check (a clear, liquid sealant that prevents fraying). Press the dart towards the centre front or back of the garment.

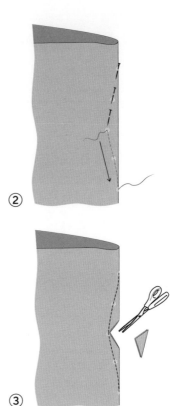

② ③

TIPS

- Bust darts are added to give shape to the bodice, so they need to be pressed carefully to keep the shaping. To do so, press the dart over a tailor's ham (or a rolled towel, or use the end of the ironing board), holding the side seam up as you press into the tip.

- If you've sewn a single dart on a heavyweight fabric that would cause a ridge if pressed to one side, cut open the fold of fabric to within 1 cm (⅜ in.) of the tip and press the dart open.

- If you have a left and a right piece, make sure the darts are the same length and are positioned in exactly the same place on each piece.

ZIPS (ZIPPERS) AND OTHER FASTENINGS

Whether they're concealed, like some zips (zippers), or make a statement, like big bold buttons, the professional finish of a garment depends to a degree on how well the fastenings have been applied. More haste, less speed should be your mantra. Take time to measure, measure and measure again, mark precisely and tack (baste) wherever you can. It will be time well spent.

ZIPS

There are three basic types of zip: conventional, open-ended and invisible.

Conventional zips have either metal or plastic teeth attached to a woven tape. The zip is closed at the base with a stopper and locks at the top. Plastic-toothed zips are usually lighter and suitable for lightweight cotton fabrics, polyester and silk. For thicker fabrics such as denim, use a metal zip.

An **open-ended**, or two-way, zip is used when a seam needs to open and close completely – on a jacket or leisurewear, for example.

In **invisible zips**, the teeth are on the underside of the zip tape with just the little zip pull showing on the right side.

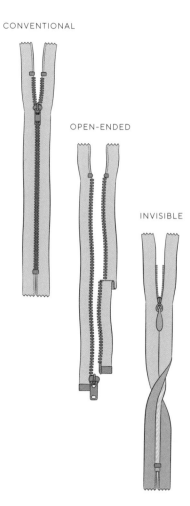

CONVENTIONAL

OPEN-ENDED

INVISIBLE

CONVENTIONAL ZIP, CENTRED

With this method, the zip sits in the centre of
the zip opening. Overlock (serge) or zigzag the
seam allowances before you insert the zip.

1 Machine tack (baste) the seam of the
garment. For a garment that has a zip
inserted partly into a seam, such as a
dress or a skirt, sew up the seam from
the hem to the zip notch on a normal
stitch length, backstitch, then machine
tack the rest of the seam. Press the seam
allowances open.

2 Place the garment wrong side up, with
the zip face down on the seam and the
zip teeth in the middle of the seam. Pin in
place, inserting the pins horizontally. If
you need a fastening such as a hook
and bar or if a waistband is going to be
attached, make sure that the zip head lies
1.5 cm (⅝ in.) below the raw edge.

3 Fit a regular zip foot to your machine.
Turn the garment over and pin the zip in
place from the right side in a U-shape,
in the direction you're going to sew. The
foot needs to sit next to the zip so that you
can stitch close to it. On some machines
the zip foot is static and you change the
needle position; on others, you can unclip
the foot and position it to the left or the
right of the needle. Indicate where you
want to cross over the bottom of the zip to
sew the other side. Mark this with a pin just
above the zip stopper.

4 Remove the pins from the wrong side of
the zip and start stitching from the top.
Pivot and stitch across the bottom, then
pivot again and stitch the other side.

5 Unpick the tacking (basting) stitches from
step 1: your zip should now sit beautifully in
the centre of the seam.

②

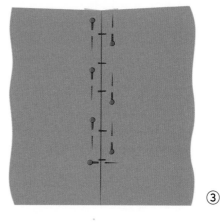

③

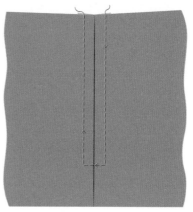

④

CONVENTIONAL ZIP, LAPPED

A lapped zip has one edge of fabric lapping the other, so that only one row of stitching is visible; the other edge is stitched very close to the zip teeth. Lapped zips are often used in side seams and in centre back seams.

1 Stitch the seam from the bottom of the zip to the garment's hemline. Press the seam open and press the seam allowance open on either side of the zip opening.

2 Working from the right side of the garment, pin the zip tape to the left-hand seam allowance, aligning the raw edges of the top of the zip tapes with the raw edge of the garment. Tack (baste) 5 mm (¼ in.) away from the teeth. Fit a regular zip foot and, with the zip open, topstitch this side of the zip, working from the bottom upwards.

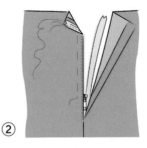

3 Close the zip and lap the unjoined side of the garment over the topstitching. Pin in place. Tack as close as you can to the teeth.

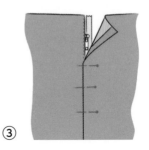

4 Using a zip foot, stitch across the bottom of the zip tapes. Leave the needle down and turn the piece so you can stitch up to the top of the zip. Remove the tacking and press with a hot iron to settle the stitches.

....

TIP

Finer fabrics can be stitched closer to the teeth; fleece or woollens should be stitched further from the teeth.

....

OPEN-ENDED ZIP

The length of the zip should equal the measurement of the jacket front from the hem to the top of the collar plus 3.5 cm (1½ in.). If the zip is too long, trim the top to this length and place a safety pin at the top to stop the pull from slipping off.

1   Close the zip. If you have trimmed the top, take care not to slide the pull off the end. With right sides together, pin the closed zip to one open edge of the jacket front and fold the upper end away from the teeth. Tack (baste) in place. Fit a zip foot and then stitch down the centre of the tape. Trim the excess tape off the top. Fold the edge of the jacket to the wrong side and finger-press so that the zip is right side out.

2   Turn the jacket inside out. With right sides together, pin the other side of the zip to the other raw edge and stitch in the same way.

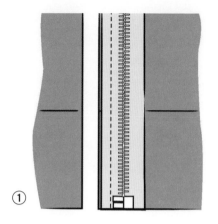

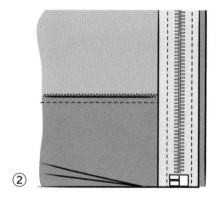

INVISIBLE ZIP

An invisible or concealed zip is sewn in place without any stitching being visible on the right side of the garment. It differs from a regular zip, as the teeth are on the underside of the zip tape with just the little zip pull showing on the right side. You will need a special invisible zip foot – a specialist foot with two angled curves on the underside, which hold the zip teeth to one side of the needle, allowing you to stitch closer to the zip than you could with any other type of foot. Invisible zips are inserted from the top down and are applied to an open seam, on the seam allowances only.

If you have a waist seam in the middle of your zip, start at step 1; if not, start at step 2.

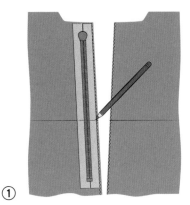

1 Position the zip tape along the centre back of the garment and make a pen mark where it matches the waist seam. The top edge of the zip tape (not the top of the functional part of the zip) should reach the top of your garment. Make a small mark on each side of the zip tape.

2 Unzip your zip and iron the teeth slightly away from the tape to make it easier to attach. Use a cool setting or the zip will melt. You can sometimes get away without this step, but it can make things easier if you are new to this method.

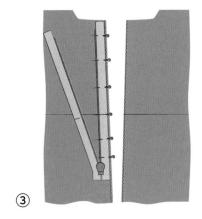

3 With the right side of the garment facing you, lay the right-hand side of the zip tape right side down on the left-hand side of the garment opening. Pin in place, matching the mark you made earlier with the waist seam (if this applies to your garment). If you are nervous about the zip moving while you sew, you can tack (baste) the zip in place at this point, either by hand or by machine.

4   Start stitching from the top by slotting the zip teeth into the left groove of the invisible zip foot. Sew as far down as you can; you will have to stop when you reach the zip pull.

5   Now position and pin the other side of the zip to the remaining side of your garment opening. Be careful not to get the zip twisted.

6   Sew from the top down by slotting the zip teeth into the right groove of the invisible zip foot.

7   Test your zip and give your garment a gentle press.

8   Close the zip. Pin the rest of the seam right sides together and stitch with a regular zip foot. You will have to start a little bit above and away from your zip stitch line to avoid the bulk of the zip pull. Also pull out the end of the zip tape so that it's not in the way.

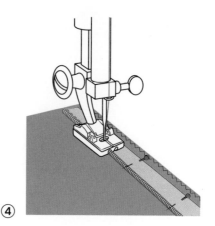

④

TIPS

- The only part of an invisible zip that you will see in your finished garment is the pull. A great tip to make the pull blend in entirely is to paint it with nail varnish.
- Always sew the zip into the opening before you stitch the seam below.
- Always sew with the zip open.

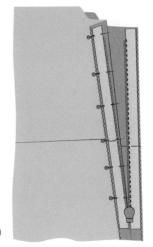

⑤

FLY ZIP

Although fly zips are a bit more fiddly than most zips, they make trousers (pants) look really professional. A fly zip is similar in construction to a lapped zip (see page 96) – it just has an additional shield stitched on the inside. In men's trousers (shown here), the fly is left over right; in women's trousers, it's right over left.

The key components of a fly zip are:

Fly facing

The facing covers the zip from view. In some patterns, it is cut as a separate piece, as shown here; in others, the facing is an extension of the centre front and is simply folded back

Fly guard

This double layer of fabric sits between you and the zip and is sewn into the right-hand side of the fly, extending underneath the opening. It stops the zip teeth from catching your skin when you pull the zip up and down.

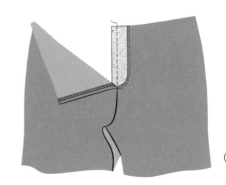

②

③

1 Overlock (serge) the crotch curves on the front trouser pieces. With right sides together, pin and sew the curve from the inside leg seam to the zip notch.

2 Interface the wrong side of the fly facing and overlock the curved edge only; try not to take any fabric off with your overlocker. Pin the fly facing on the right-hand side of the trouser front (as you look at it), right sides together. Pin and sew from the waist to the zip notch.

3 Press the facing away from the right trouser leg, then trim the seam allowance and press it away from the trouser leg as well. Place the zip face down on the facing, aligning the bottom of the zip with the zip notch. Align the side of the zip with the seam that joins the facing to the trousers. Sew the left side of the zip to the facing, then fold the facing towards the inside of the trousers and press lightly.

4 Fold the fly guard in half, right sides together. Sew the short curved edge, trim and clip the seam allowance, then turn right side out. Overlock the longest straight edge.

5 Open the zip. Place the trousers right side up, then press 5 mm (¼ in.) to the wrong side on the left-hand side trouser front (as you look at it). Tack (baste) the zip in place behind the fold; you should only see the zip teeth. Position the fly guard behind the trousers, aligning the overlocked edge with the edge of the zip tape, and stitch close to the trouser front fold through all three layers (trousers, zip and fly guard).

6 Turn the trousers over so that you can see the inside. Pin the fly guard out of the way to prepare for topstitching. Close the zip and turn the trousers right side up again.

7 Draw a topstitching curve that matches the shape of the fly facing underneath and sew through the trousers and the facing.

8 Unpin the fly guard so that it sits over the zip. Pin the fly guard in position where it wants to sit. From the front of the trousers, bar tack at the very bottom of the topstitched line and also at the start of the curve (see Tips). These stitches will go through all layers: trousers, zip, facing and fly guard. If the zip is too long, trim it above the waist seam allowance.

TIPS

∘ A bar tack is simply a series of zigzag stitches placed very close together. Set a standard zigzag stitch 2–3mm (¹⁄₁₆–⅛ in.) wide and stitch a short row 1–2 cm (⅜–¾ in.) long. Backstitch once or twice over the entire row to secure.

∘ If you need to cut the zip to create the right length for your garment, hand sew a tack across the top before you cut so that you don't accidentally pull the zip head entirely out of the zip before it's been sewn in.

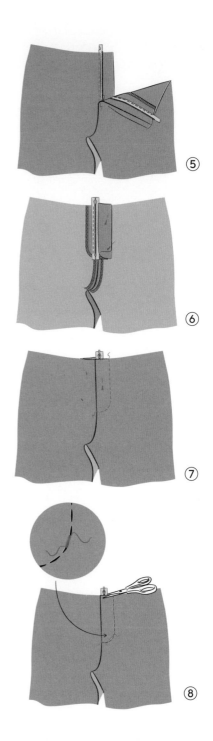

BUTTONS AND BUTTONHOLES

Badly stitched buttonholes ruin any garment, so the key is to practise on spare fabric. Make up the layers of fabric as they appear on the garment (usually a folded piece) so that you can test the buttonhole setting on your sewing machine. First, however, you'll need to mark the buttonhole positions.

POSITIONING BUTTONHOLES AND BUTTONS

The centre front of your buttoned-up garment will lie somewhere along the middle of the button stand (the area of the garment that holds the buttons on one side and the buttonholes on the other). This should be indicated on your pattern. When you overlap the button stands, the centre front lines will lie on top of each other. The buttons and buttonholes will be positioned along this line.

° Buttons go on top of the centre front line.

° Horizontal buttonholes should start 3 mm (⅛ in.) from the centre line towards the edge of the garment.

° Vertical buttonholes go on top of the centre line.

Sewing patterns are usually marked with the buttonhole positions **(1)**, but if yours is not or you want to change the positions to some that are more flattering to your figure, measure and mark them carefully. Buttonholes should be at least 1–2 cm (⅜–¾ in.) from the fabric edge and 5–8 cm (2–3 in.) apart, depending on the fabric weight and style of the garment.

Use a sewing gauge to check your positioning. Use the sliding marker to ensure all the buttonhole positions are evenly spaced and at exactly the same position in from the edge of the opening **(2)**.

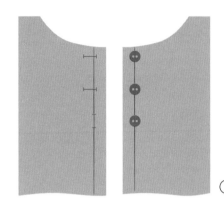

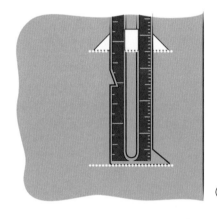

STITCHING BUTTONHOLES

Modern machines will either sew a buttonhole in one step or, on basic models, in four steps. Many now come with a buttonhole foot with a slot in the back for the button, so that the hole is the perfect size.

Prepare the fabric by interfacing the buttonhole section. On very lightweight fabrics, add an extra layer of tearaway stabilizer below each buttonhole area.

BUTTONHOLE FOOT WITH SLOT FOR BUTTON

1 Insert the button into the back of the foot, following the manufacturer's instructions.

2 Snap on the buttonhole foot and bring down the buttonhole lever. Set the sewing machine to your chosen buttonhole stitch, which is usually a one-step buttonhole when this foot is supplied.

3 Position the garment under the foot, with the needle ready to insert into the correct end of buttonhole placement mark (which end of buttonhole depends on which way your machine stitches). Once stitched, feed the thread tails through to the back of the work and then through the close stitching of one side before cutting them off.

4 Place a pin at one end of the buttonhole so that you don't accidentally cut through the end bar. Starting at the other end, use a seam ripper or a pair of small, sharp scissors to open the buttonhole.

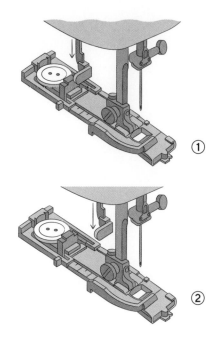

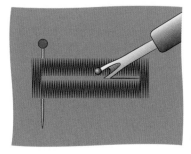

FOUR-STEP BUTTONHOLE

1 Attach the buttonhole foot and select step 1 of the buttonhole sequence. (You may need to adjust the stitch length down to virtually 0, too.) Stitch the first end bar tack. Once complete, the machine will stop ready for you to turn the dial to step 2 to stitch the left side of the buttonhole.

2 Stitch the length needed, stopping at the marked line you made for your buttonhole size. Turn the dial back to step 1 for the second bar tack. Then turn the dial to stitch the right-hand side, stitching until you reach the first bar tack. Take threads to the back and tie off. Open the buttonhole, as in step 4 on page 103.

TIPS

° Button stands can either be 'grown on' (part of the front garment pattern) or attached separately.

° On men's garments, the buttonholes go on the left button stand; on women's garments, they go on the right.

° If your machine does not have a foot that fits a button in the back, you will have to work out the buttonhole size yourself. Measure flat buttons across the width and add 3 mm (⅛ in.). For domed buttons, measure the circumference and add 3 mm (⅛ in.). If you are using very thick buttons, make the buttonhole slightly bigger.

° Always have an odd number of buttons, as this works better for positioning.

° Buttons never go all the way down on a garment. Look at jackets and button-down shirts in your wardrobe and see where the last button is positioned.

SEWING ON BUTTONS BY HAND

Depending on where they are, buttons can take considerable strain so make sure they're all sewn on very firmly. Use doubled thread (or topstitch thread, which is a little thicker and stronger than general-purpose sewing thread) and go through the holes at least four times. This is the way to sew on a button with a thread shank to allow for heavier fabrics. If you're sewing buttons onto a shirt or any other garment made of fine fabric, the buttons won't need a shank, so just sew the button on without using the hairgrip (bobby pin) spacer or winding the thread around underneath the button.

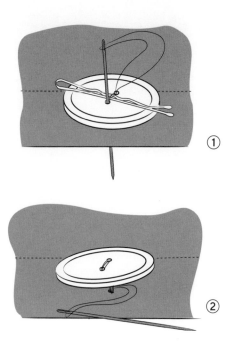

1   Hold the button in position and bring the needle up from under the fabric and through one hole in the button. Place a match or hairgrip across the button between the holes and pass the needle down through the second hole. Repeat four times. If your button has four holes, work the stitches in a cross.

2   Once the button is firmly sewn in position, pass the needle down through one hole but not through the fabric, then remove the match or hairgrip. Make a thread shank by winding the thread around the stitches, between the button and the fabric. Finally, pass the needle through to the wrong side of the fabric and secure with several tiny stitches on top of each other.

COVERED BUTTONS

It's sometimes hard to find exactly the right buttons for your garments, but covered buttons mean the sky's the limit: you can use a small-patterned fabric for buttons on a solid-coloured garment, or pick out one colour from your fabric and really let the buttons stand out.

The easiest way to cover buttons is to use a kit. There are plenty available in various sizes from haberdashery (notions) departments or online. The best consist of the button tops, button backs (which include shanks), a mould and a pusher. The kit will also include a circular cardboard template.

1   Using the correct-size template, cut out a circle of fabric for each button. Place a button top on one of the circles.

2   Place this ensemble in the mould and fold over the raw edges of the fabric into the middle.

3   Place the button back on top.

4   Place the pusher on top of this and gently press down until the button back clicks into position.

HOOKS

Small and generally concealed, hooks play a remarkably important part in keeping garments securely fastened. Tiny hooks and eyes at the top of a zip (zipper) stop it from opening, while more robust hooks and bars at the waistline of trousers (pants) and skirts can take immense strain. As with all fastenings, measuring and marking to ensure the correct position is extremely important. Whatever the size, the hook should be stitched onto the overlap and the bar or eye onto the underlying section.

1 Start with the bar: if it's at the top of a zip, then position it directly above the teeth so that it can take all the strain. Use doubled thread knotted at the end. Bring the needle up from the underside and up through the hole at one end of the bar, then pass the needle back down through the fabric outside the hole. Repeat three times and secure with two tiny stitches at the back. Repeat with the hole at the other end of the bar, making sure the bar is precisely vertical.

2 Hook the hook over the bar and lay the flap over it to ensure it is in the correct position. Holding the hook in position, sew it to the under layer of the top flap so that the stitches don't show on the front of the garment.

FABRIC TIES AND BELTS

Fabric ties and belts are used on many garments and are often made from the same fabric as the garment. They are cut on the straight grain (see page 62).

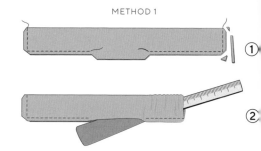

TIP

If you want your ties to have some firmness, interface half the width (see page 72).

METHOD 1

This is the standard method for tie belts, and has the seam along the bottom edge and the fold at the top edge.

1 Interface half the tie fabric if required. Once cooled, fold the tie fabric in half lengthways, right sides together, with the raw edges together. Starting at one short end and taking a 1.5-cm (⅝-in.) seam allowance, stitch across the end, pivot, and stitch along the long edge, leaving a turning gap of about 20 cm (8 in.) in the middle, then continue to the other end, pivoting to stitch the other short end. Trim the seam allowance, leaving the turning gap seam allowance untrimmed. Cut the corners off at an angle, close to the stitching.

2 Turn the tie right side out, pushing the stitched ends through to the opening in the centre with a ruler or other blunt tool. Once turned through, use a point turner to ease out the corners completely.

3 Turn in the raw edges of the turning gap and slipstitch them closed. Press, with the seam on the lower edge of the tie.

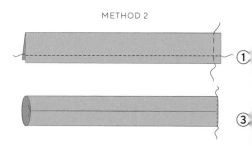

METHOD 2

Use this method to conceal the seam at the centre back of the tie.

1 Fold the tie fabric in half lengthways, right sides together, with the raw edges together. Stitch along the long edge. Tack (baste) across one short end.

2 Turn the tie through to the right side from the tacked end, pushing the end through with a ruler as in step 2 of Method 1.

3 Unpick the tacking stitches and roll the tube in your fingers so that the seam runs along the centre. Tuck in the seam allowance at each short end and either edge stitch by machine or slipstitch the opening closed.

METHOD 3

This is a very quick method of making straps and ties, and is particularly useful for fabrics that are thick or difficult to turn through.

1 With the wrong side uppermost, fold one long edge of the tie to the wrong side by 1 cm (⅜ in.) and press. Fold the other long edge to the centre of the tie and press. Fold the neatened edge to the centre, overlapping the raw edge of the other side. Stitch down the centre close to the fold. Stitch again down either long edge an equal distance from the centre stitching and edges.

2 Turn under the raw ends and edge stitch by machine.

ROULEAU LOOPS

These are narrow ties used as straps on lingerie, to create button loops or as inner ties on a dressing gown. They can be tricky to turn through, but there are two methods that make it easier.

METHOD 1 – SHOELACE

1 Cut the fabric strip to the width required. Fold the fabric in half, right sides together, and then insert a shoelace or piece of string at least 5 cm (2 in.) longer than the strip into the folded fabric. Centre the shoelace at one end, then tack (baste) across that end Then stitch the long edge, backstitching at the start and finish.

2 Trim the seam allowance and pull on the shoelace to pull the fabric right side out. You may have to start off the tacked end by pushing it inside by hand first.

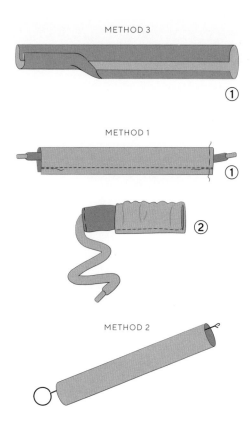

METHOD 3

①

METHOD 1

①

②

METHOD 2

3 Remove the tacking stitches at the end of the tie and take out the shoelace.

METHOD 2 – ROULEAU LOOP TURNER

A rouleau loop turner is a long metal rod with a loop and tiny latched hook at one end. Having stitched the long edges of the tie together, insert the loop turner, pushing it right to the other end of the tie and hook a little of the fabric onto the hook. Help start turning it through at that end, and then pull on the loop turner to bring the fabric through to the right side.

PRESS STUDS (SNAPS)

Amazingly strong for their size, press studs (snap fasteners) can be used to close a whole opening, or used at the top of an otherwise buttoned opening. They consist of two parts: a ball and a socket, both with four or six sewing holes around the circumference and a central hole, which can be used as an alignment aid. Start by measuring and marking the position of the ball part on the garment.

1   The ball part goes onto the underside of the overlapping part of the garment, so you need to carefully sew it to the facing or fold back to ensure the stitches don't show at the front. Position the centre of the press stud over the marked position and stitch through the holes around the press studs.

2   To position the socket, pass a needle through the central hole in the ball part and use that to align the ball with the hole in the centre of the socket part, held in position on the other side of the opening. Hold the socket part in position as you remove the needle from the alignment holes, then stitch the socket in position.

NO-SEW FASTENINGS

Jeans buttons, heavy-duty snaps and rivets used on worker wear and casual clothing are now available as kits for home sewers. They are not sewn in position; instead, they are securely riveted or hammered home. To attach some no-sew fastenings, all you need is a hammer. Others come complete with their own tool set, which is essentially a small mould and a tool to secure the fastening in position. Each is slightly different, although all come with instructions.

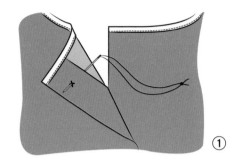

①

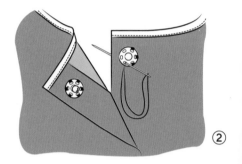

②

APPLYING JEANS BUTTONS

Jeans buttons come in two parts: a tack for the underside of the fabric and the button for the top. Work a buttonhole in the same way as for any other button (see page 102).

Start by marking the position of the button. Now push the point of the tack up through the fabric from the underside. Place it on a flat surface and position the button piece over the point of the tack. Gently hammer the button home using a light hammer.

SLEEVES

T-SHIRT SLEEVE

T-shirt sleeves have a shallow sleeve head (the curved section where the top of the sleeve meets the shoulder seam) and are attached to the armhole before the side and underarm seams are sewn.

1 Pin and sew the front to the back at the shoulder seams, then press the shoulder seams towards the back.

2 Lay the garment flat, right side up. With right sides together, matching the double notches on the sleeve with those on the back of the armhole, and the single notches with those on the front of the armhole, pin the sleeves all around the armhole. Stitch in place.

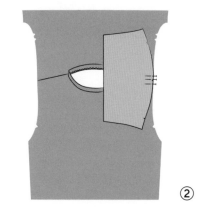

TIP

The armhole and sleeve curve in opposite directions, so you may need to ease them together as you pin. Horizontal pinning is perfect for this.

3 Fold the garment in half at the shoulders, right sides together. Pin the side and underarm seams, matching the side notches, the bottom hem and the sleeve ends. Stitch from the hem to the end of the sleeve on each side.

SET-IN SLEEVE

Set-in sleeves are often used on blouses, shirts, jackets and coats .The sleeve head needs to fit into the armhole and curve over the shoulder. To do this, the sleeve head has to be cut larger than the armhole and then gathered or 'eased' to fit. Before you insert the sleeves, stitch, press and finish any seams that intersect the garment's armholes.

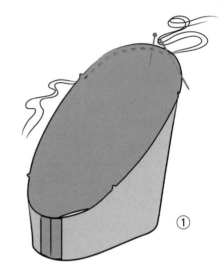

1   With right sides together, pin the underarm seam of each sleeve and stitch. Press the seams open and finish the raw edges. Fold the sleeves in half lengthways and mark the centre top with a pin. At the sleeve heads, run gathering stitches (see page 83) between the marks that you transferred from the pattern piece.

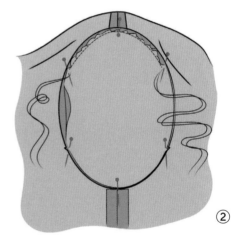

2   Turn the garment inside out and the sleeves right side out. With right sides together, slip the sleeves through the armholes, matching up the notches and matching underarm seams with side seams and the top pin with the shoulder seams. Pin at these points. Gently pull up the gathering stitches to fit the sleeve head in the armhole, arranging the fullness evenly. Tack (baste) the sleeve into the armhole using small stitches, and then stitch in place, beginning and ending at the underarm seam and overlapping the ends of the stitching. Remove the tacking stitches, then trim and neaten the seam allowances. Press the armhole seams towards the sleeve, working the tip of the iron along the curve of the seam.

ONE-PIECE RAGLAN SLEEVE

A raglan sleeve has a diagonal seam that runs from the underarm up to the collarbone; it covers the entire shoulder. In a one-piece raglan sleeve, a dart is stitched at the neck edge to provide some shaping over the shoulders. Before you insert the sleeves, stitch, press and finish any seams that intersect the garment's armholes.

1 Stitch the shoulder dart (see page 92), then stitch the shoulder seam. Press the dart and the underarm seam open.

2 With right sides together, stitch the garment side seams.

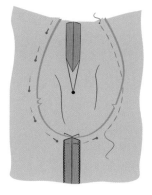

3 Turn the garment wrong side out and the sleeve right side out. With right sides together, matching the neck edges and pattern notches, and matching the underarm seams to the garment side seams, pin and tack (baste) the sleeve into the armhole.

4 Working from the sleeve side, stitch the sleeve in place. Remove the tacking stitches. Reinforce the seam with a second row of stitches between the underarm notches, stitching within the seam allowance.

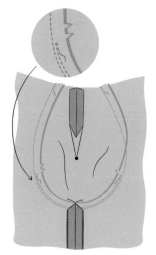

5 Trim the seam allowances to reduce bulk. Finish the seam allowances together, then press them towards the sleeves.

TWO-PIECE RAGLAN SLEEVE

In a two-piece raglan sleeve, a seam that runs across the shoulder and down the outer arm provides the shaping.

1 With right sides together, pin the front and back sleeve pieces together along the shoulder and outer seams.

2 Stitch the whole seam, then notch the seam allowances along the shoulder curve. Press the seam open.

....

TIP

Raglan sleeves are often used on sport and leisurewear, as they have a loose fit. For a sporty, casual look, try making the sleeves in a contrasting colour to the front and back of the top.

....

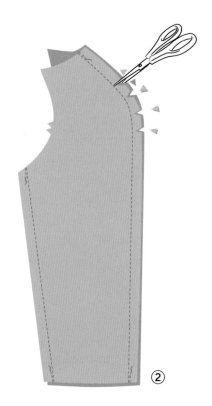

②

SLEEVE FINISHES

Depending on the style of your garment, there are various ways of finishing a sleeve, from an easy-to-stitch turned-up hem to a neat cuff.

SELF-HEM

The easiest way to finish a sleeve end, of course, is with a simple hem. This method gives a flat, almost invisible finish.

1   If you wish, first trim the sleeve seam allowances in half between the hemline and the raw edge to reduce bulk.

2   Zigzag stitch the raw edge of the sleeve end, then turn it to the wrong side and pin or tack (baste) it in place just below the zigzag stitching.

3   Blind hem by hand or by machine (see page 90). Remove the tacking stitches.

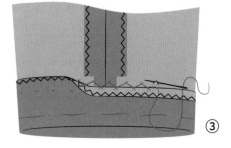

VARIATION

Use elastic to gather the sleeve end. Cut a piece of elastic to fit your wrist, plus 1.5 cm (⅝ in.). To work out the depth of the hem, add 1 cm (⅜ in.) to the width of the elastic. Turn up the sleeve end by this amount, press in a crease and unfold. Fold 5 mm (¼ in.) to the wrong side along the raw edge and press. Fold up the hem along the crease, pin in place, then machine stitch close to the folded top edge, leaving a gap at the underarm seam. Insert the elastic into the gap, then stitch the gap closed (see Applied casing, page 116, steps 4 and 5). For a really neat finish, machine stitch around the bottom edge of the hem, too.

APPLIED CASING

In this method, a separate strip of fabric is stitched onto the end of the sleeve and folded to the wrong side, then elastic is inserted to gather the sleeve end. This technique is useful if you've accidentally cut the sleeve too short for a normal turned-up hem.

②

1   Cut a piece of elastic to fit your wrist, plus about 1.5 cm (⅝ in.). Measure the circumference of the sleeve end, then cut a strip of fabric 2 cm (¾ in.) longer than this and 2 cm (¾ in.) wider than the elastic. Press 1 cm (⅜ in.) to the wrong side at each short end, and 5 mm (¼ in.) to the wrong side on each long edge.

2   Unfold one long edge, then pin it to the end of the sleeve, with right sides together. The casing ends should meet at the underarm seam. Machine stitch along the crease.

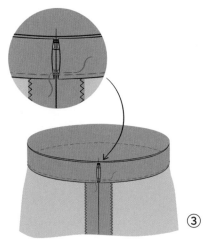

③

3   Fold the casing to the wrong side of the sleeve and press. Pin the casing to the sleeve and machine stitch it in place, leaving a small opening at the underarm seam.

4   Attach a safety pin to one end of the elastic, then feed it through the gap in the casing. Overlap the ends by about 1.5 cm (⅝ in.), then stitch them together.

5   Hand stitch the gap in the casing closed.

④

OPENINGS FOR CLOSE-FITTING CUFFS

Cuffs that fit snugly around the wrist need an opening at the end of the sleeve for the wearer to slip their hand through; make this opening before you stitch the sleeve's underarm seam and attach the cuff.

FACED CUFF OPENING

In this method, a rectangle of fabric (a facing) is stitched over the area where the sleeve end is to be slit, neatly finishing the raw edges. Cut the facing about 6.5 cm (2 ½ in.) wide and 2.5 cm (1 in.) longer than the slit.

1 Fold under and press 6 mm (¼ in.) to the wrong side along both long edges and one short edge of each facing strip. Machine stitch in place. Mark the position of the slit on the facing.

2 With right sides together, pin the facing over the end of the sleeve, matching up the marked slits on both pieces. Working from the facing side, stitch closely around the marked slit line in a V shape. Carefully cut up the middle of the slit, making sure you don't cut through the stitches at the top.

3 Turn the facing to the wrong side of the sleeve and press. Tack (baste) the bottom edge of the facing in place, ready to attach the cuff. Stitch the facing to the sleeve, close to the edges; you can either machine stitch it in place or slipstitch by hand (see page 82). Press carefully.

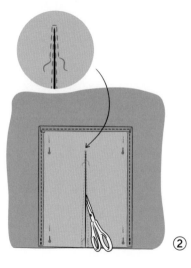

SHIRT SLEEVE PLACKET OPENING

This consists of two pieces of fabric for each sleeve – a sleeve placket and a sleeve binding – that overlap, allowing the cuff to fit closely around the wrist. The overlap piece (the placket) has a shaped top end; the underlap piece (the binding) has a straight top end.

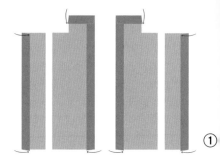

1   Fold under 1 cm (⅜ in.) to the wrong side on one long edge of each sleeve placket and placket binding piece, and press. Fold under and press the top edge of each sleeve placket piece by 1 cm (⅜ in.), too. Be sure to make a mirrored set!

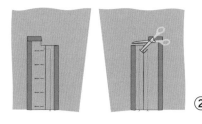

2   Lay the sleeves out, wrong side up, and cut the marked slit on each one. Place the placket pieces and placket bindings wrong side up on each side of the slit, remembering to mirror their positions on the second sleeve. Pin in place and stitch along each side to the top of the slit. Cut from the top of the slit towards either side of the stitched edges to form a Y shape.

3   Turn the placket piece though the slash line to the right side of the sleeve. Wrap the placket binding around the raw edge of that side of the slit, encasing the stitching. Press, pin and topstitch close to the original seamline.

4   Fold the placket in half, wrong sides together, making sure you cover the line of stitching, and press. Pin and topstitch in place, starting at the hem edge.

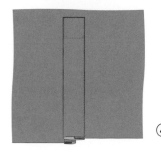

....

TIP

Place the placket binding on the side of the slit nearest the back of the sleeve and the sleeve placket on the side of the slit nearest the front of the sleeve.

....

CUFFS

Cuffs may be made of either one or two parts. They are interfaced to provide some rigidity.

LOOSE-FITTING CUFFS

Loose-fitting cuffs require no opening – the pieces are large enough for your hand and arm to fit through comfortably. The cuff pattern piece is marked with a central foldline.

1   Gather the end of the sleeve to fit the cuff, if necessary.

2   Fold the cuff in half, wrong sides together, and press to form a crease. Open up. Apply interfacing to the wrong side, up to the crease. With right sides together, pin, tack (baste) and machine stitch the short ends together to form a tube. Press the seam open.

3   On the non-interfaced end of the cuff, press the seam allowance to the wrong side and tack in place.

4   With right sides together, matching the cuff and underarm seams, pin the interfaced edge of the cuff to the sleeve end. Machine stitch. Trim the corners of the cuff seam allowance diagonally, then grade (see page 44) to reduce bulk.

5   Pull the cuff down and press the seam allowances towards the cuff. Turn the sleeve wrong side out. On the inside of the sleeve, fold back the tacked edge of the cuff to align with the previous line of stitching, then slipstitch it in place.

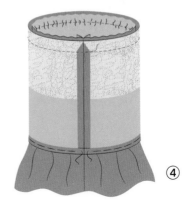

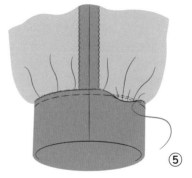

CLOSE-FITTING CUFFS

1 If your cuff is just one piece, apply interfacing up to the central foldline. If it is two pieces, interface one piece. Along the top edge, turn and press the seam allowance to the wrong side on the non-interfaced section of a one-piece cuff and on the non-interfaced piece of a two-piece cuff. Tack (baste) in place.

2 On a one-piece cuff, fold the piece in half, right sides together, and stitch the side edges together. On a two-piece cuff, pin the two pieces right sides together, aligning the raw edges. Stitch along the side and lower edges. Grade the seam allowances (see page 44), trim the corners and turn right side out.

3 Stitch the underarm seam of the sleeve and press the seam open. Finish the seam allowances separately.

4 With right sides together, matching the notch on the cuff with the sleeve seam, pin the cuff to the end of the sleeve. The front edge of the sleeve opening should be level with the cuff; the back of the cuff will extend beyond the sleeve opening,. Tack and machine stitch in place. Trim and grade the seam allowances.

5 Pull the cuff down and press the seam allowances towards the cuff. Bring the loose, tacked edge of the cuff in line with the machine stitching on the inside of the sleeve and slipstitch in place.

6 Work a buttonhole on the overlap of the cuff and sew a button to the underlap (see pages 102 and 105).

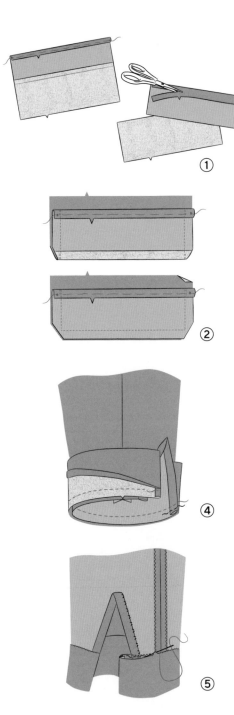

① ② ④ ⑤

SLEEVE TABS

Sleeve tabs are a neat way of rolling up long sleeves to elbow length or slightly above. If they're not included in your pattern, cut four rectangles twice the depth of your cuff turn-up plus 5 cm (2 in.) by 5 cm (2 in.). Sew the tabs in place before you sew up the sleeves.

1 Interface two of the fabric rectangles. Shape one short end of each rectangle into a V shape or a curve. For each tab, place an interfaced and a non-interfaced rectangle right sides together and sew all around with a 1-cm (⅜-in.) seam allowance, leaving a gap in one long edge for turning.

2 Clip the corners, grade the seam allowances (see page 44) and turn right side out. Fold in the edges of the gap, then topstitch all around, close to the edge. Work a vertical buttonhole in the shaped short end (see page 102).

3 Decide how far down the sleeve you want the tab to fasten. On the wrong side of your sleeve, measure this distance from the centre notch and move over about 2.5 cm (1 in.) from here towards the front of the sleeve. The front of the sleeve will be marked by a single notch; the back by a double notch. Mark this point. Centre the straight end of your tab on the mark and stitch around the straight end in a square shape.

4 On the right side of the sleeve, hand stitch a button over the stitched square that holds the tab in place.

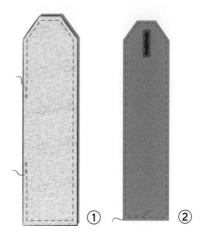

POCKETS

Pockets should be strong enough to withstand a bit of wear and tear so, whatever type you're making, it's a good idea to reinforce the openings or top corners by backstitching over the end of the seam.

UNLINED PATCH POCKET

Patch pockets are usually made from the same fabric as the garment, but if you want them to stand out you can use a contrasting fabric or decorate them with appliqué motifs or embroidery before you sew them in place. For extra body, apply interfacing from the top of the pocket down to the foldline marked on the pattern.

1 Overlock (serge) or zigzag the top raw edge of the pocket, then tack (baste) around the seamline as a guide to where to fold under the seam allowance later.

2 Fold over the top edge of the pocket to the right side (the foldline will be marked on your pattern) and pin in place, making sure that the notches match and the raw side edges align. Stitch across the folded section only, then carefully snip off the top corners.

3 Turn the folded top section right side out and use a pin to gently push out the corners to a sharp point.

①

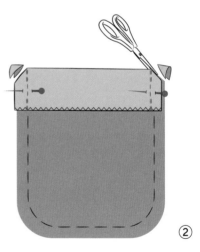

②

4 Turn the raw side and bottom edges to the wrong side along the tacked seamline and press. If the bottom of the pocket is curved, ease the curve into a smooth line. Tack the turned-under edges in place if you wish.

5 Pin the pocket to the garment, then topstitch it in place. You can work a second line of topstitching just inside the first for extra strength if you wish. It's also a good idea to reinforce the top corners by backstitching or zigzagging for 1.5 cm (⅝ in.) or so, as these are the areas that take the most wear and tear.

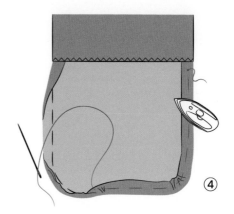

④

TIP

Place the pins at right angles to the seam, so that you can stitch the pocket in place without having to remove them.

⑤

PATCH POCKET FLAP

Attach the flap after you have sewn the pocket in place, to ensure that you get the spacing right.

1 Pin two pocket flap pieces right sides together, then sew along the short sides and the shaped edge. Trim the seam allowance and clip into the corners. Turn right side out, using a bamboo pointer or a knitting needle to get neat, sharp corners, and press.

2 Overlock (serge) or zigzag the open edge. Topstitch all around. Make a vertical buttonhole close to the point of the V shape (see page 103).

3 Place the flap upside down above the pocket, with the overlocked/zigzagged edge about 1 cm (⅜ in.) away from the pocket's top edge. Sew along the overlocked edge, then press the flap down into its correct position and topstitch 5 mm (¼ in.) away from the top edge to hold the flap down.

4 Mark the button position through the buttonhole, then sew a button to the pocket (see page 105).

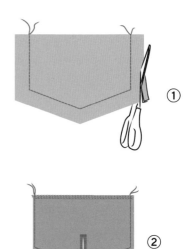

IN-SEAM POCKET

This type of pocket is often used in the side seams of loose-fitting skirts and trousers (pants). Sometimes the pockets are cut as separate pieces, as shown here; in other patterns, the pockets are extensions of the front and back garment pieces and the pocket is stitched as one with the garment seam, following steps 4 and 5, below.

1 Staystitch (see page 83) the upper edge of the front and back trouser pieces, stitching just inside the seam allowance.

2 With right sides together and the straight edge of the pocket along the raw edge of the garment, pin one pocket piece to the front of the garment at the position shown on the pattern. Sew in place along the seamline. Repeat on the back garment section.

3 Trim the seam allowances and neaten the raw edges of the pockets with a zigzag or overedge stitch. Press the pocket pieces away from the garment along the stitching line.

4 Place the front and back of the garment right sides together, matching up the pockets. Pin the side seams and the pocket (which extends beyond the garment). Stitch the side seam, pivoting at the top of the pocket and continuing around the pocket bag, and pivoting again down the garment seam.

5 Snip into the seam allowance of the back garment piece at the pivot points. Neaten the garment seam allowances separately and the pocket seam allowances together. Press the garment seams open and press the pocket towards the front of the garment.

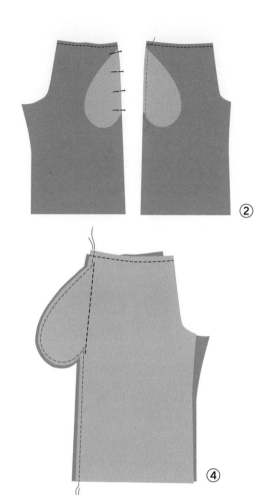

FRONT HIP POCKET

Often used on jeans, leisurewear and skirts, a front hip pocket consists of two separate pieces: a pocket back and a pocket facing. The pocket back is cut from fabric and the pocket facing from lining.

1   Apply a 2.5-cm- (1-in.)-wide strip of interfacing to the wrong side of the garment's pocket opening edge and the opening edge of the pocket facing (see page 72).

2   With right sides together, matching the waist and side seam edges, pin and tack (baste) the pocket facing to the garment front. Machine stitch in place, backstitching at the start and finish.

3   Trim and layer the seam allowances and notch the curves (see page 87). Press the seam allowances towards the facing. Understitch the seam allowances to the facing (see page 83).

4   Press the facing to the wrong side of the garment front. If you wish, topstitch the pocket opening edges for decoration.

5   With right sides together, pin and stitch the pocket back to the pocket facing around the long curved edge. Neaten the seam allowances together.

6   Tack the pocket to the garment front and the waist and side seam edges. Reinforce both ends of the pocket opening with zigzag stitching just outside the waist and side seam stitchlines, then make up the rest of the garment as normal.

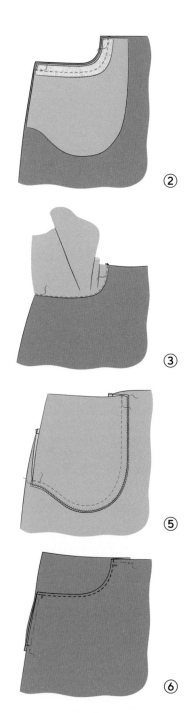

②
③
⑤
⑥

COLLARS

Although there are many variations in shape and finish, most collars fall into two main categories: flat and stand (or shirt).

FLAT COLLAR

Flat collars are made up of two layers: the top collar, which is the side that's on view when the garment is worn, and the under collar, which is the side that sits next to the neckline of the garment. If the garment opens at the front, there will be one collar piece for each layer, fitting all the way round the neckline, as shown here; if it opens at the back, there will be two collar pieces for each layer. The method for attaching them is the same.

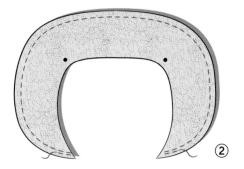

1   Staystitch the neck edge of the garment (see page 83). Press and neaten any darts or seams that intersect the neckline. If the garment has a zip (zipper) that opens at the neckline, insert it before you attach the collar.

2   Interface the wrong side of the under collar (see pagr 72). With right sides together, aligning the raw edges, pin and stitch the top and under collars together, leaving the neck edge open.

3   Trim and grade the seam allowances (see page 87), snip the corners diagonally and notch any curved seam allowances.

4 Turn the collar right side out and press. Pin and tack (baste) the open neck edges together.

5 Matching any pattern markings and making sure that the top (non-interfaced) collar is uppermost, pin and tack the collar to the neckline of the right side of the garment.

6 Make up the neck facing and attach it to the garment, sandwiching the collar in between (see page 131). With the facing right side up, understitch the seam allowances to the facing around the neckline. Press the facing to the inside of the garment. Slipstitch the lower edge of the facing to the shoulder seams (for a garment that opens at the front) or to the zip (zipper) tape (for a garment that has a zip in the centre back).

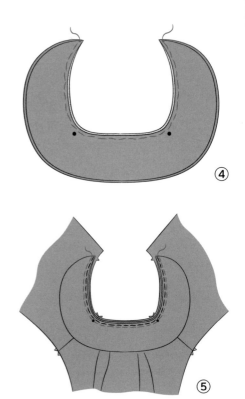

STAND (SHIRT) COLLAR

A stand collar pattern consists of a collar piece and a collar stand that allows for a tie to be fastened under the collar. Cut two collar pieces and two stands.

....

TIP

In some patterns the collar and stand are cut separately, as shown here; in others, the stand is an extension of the collar. The method for attaching them is the same.

....

1 Staystitch the neck edge of the garment (see page 83). Stitch the shoulder seams, finish the seam allowances and press the seams open. Apply interfacing to the wrong side of the under collar and one stand piece.

2 With right sides together, pin, tack (baste) and machine stitch the top and under collar pieces together along the side and upper edges. Trim and grade the seam allowances, and snip the corners diagonally (see page 87).

3 Turn the collar right side out and push the corners out. Press, then topstitch the finished edges if you wish (see page 83).

4 On the non-interfaced stand piece, fold up the seam allowance along the neck edge only. Pin and tack this edge close to the fold, then trim the seam allowance down to 6 mm (¼ in.).

5 With the under collar against the right side of the interfaced stand piece, pin and tack along the open edges of the collar; the stand will extend beyond the collar at each end.

6 Place the non-interfaced stand piece right side down on top, aligning the raw edges, so that the collar is sandwiched in between. Machine stitch, starting and finishing at the pressed edge of the interfaced stand piece. Remove the tacking stitches and grade the seam allowances (see page 87). Turn the piece right side out.

7 With right sides together, pin and tack the interfaced side of the collar stand to the neckline of the garment. Machine stitch, then grade and clip the seam allowances.

8 Press the neck seam up towards the collar stand. Bring the tacked edge of the non-interfaced stand piece down to meet the seamline and slipstitch it neatly in place.

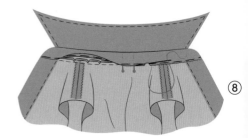

FACINGS

Facings are used to neaten and finish off the edges on armholes, necklines and waists, instead of collars, sleeves and waistbands. They are also found on the front openings of many blouses and jackets or coats. They are usually cut from the same fabric as the garment and interfaced to add support. Once attached, a facing is turned to the inside of a garment, so that it is invisible from the outside.

NECK FACING

Regardless of the neckline shape – round, square, sweetheart or V-shape – the construction of a neck facing is much the same. It may consist of a front and back facing, as shown here, or (if the garment has a centre back opening) of one front and two back facings. Sew the shoulder seams of the garment before you attach the neck facing.

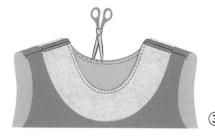

1   Apply interfacing to the front and back neck facings. With right sides together, pin the front and back neck facings together at the shoulder seams. Machine stitch.

2   Neaten the seam allowances and press the seams open. Neaten the lower edge of the facing with a zigzag stitch or an edge stitch, or on an overlocker (serger).

3   Lay the garment flat, right side up. Lay the facing right side down on top, matching up the raw edges of the

neckline and the shoulder seams. Pin, then sew around the neckline. (If the neckline is curved, as shown here, sew slowly and clip the neckline curve (see page 87).

4   Press both the facing and the seam allowances away from the body of the garment. Understitch (see page 83) the facing around the neckline, stitching only through the facing and the seam allowance. Secure the facing to the shoulder seam allowance of the garment with a few small hand stitches.

ARMHOLE FACING

An armhole facing is one way of finishing a sleeveless blouse or dress; alternatively, you can bind the armhole edges (see page 148). It is constructed and applied in much the same way as a neck facing. Sew the shoulder and side seams of the garment before you attach the facings.

1   Apply interfacing to the wrong sides of the front and back armhole facings. With right sides together, pin and stitch a front facing to a back facing along both short ends to form a loop. Repeat with the other front and back facing. Press the seams open. Zigzag stitch or overlock (serge) the outer edges of the facings.

2   With right sides together, matching the notches and matching the garment side and shoulder seams to the seam on the facings, pin the facings around the armholes. Machine stitch in place, then clip into the seam allowances to make sure you get a flat curve.

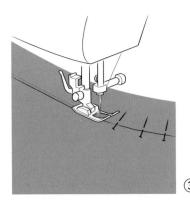

3   Open out the facings and press the seam allowances towards the facings and away from the garment. Working from the right side, understitch the facings 3 mm (⅛ in.) away from the seam (see page 83).

4   Turn the facing inside the armholes and press around the edge, making sure that the seam and understitching are 'rolled' towards the inside. Using a simple hand stitch, catch the facings to the seam allowances of the garments at the shoulders and at the armholes.

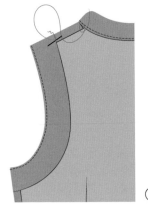

COMBINED NECK AND ARMHOLE FACING

This is a great way to finish the neckline and armholes of a garment at the same time. It can be used for any sleeveless garment that has a seam at the centre back. Sew the shoulder seams of the garment before you attach the facing.

1   Apply interfacing to the front and back neck facings. With right sides together, pin the front and back neck facings together at the shoulder seams. Machine stitch. Neaten the lower edge of the facing with a zigzag stitch or an edge stitch, or on an overlocker (serger).

2   Lay the garment flat, right side up. Lay the facing right side down on top, matching up the raw edges of the neckline and the shoulder seams. Pin, then sew around the neckline.

3   If the neckline is curved, as here, clip the neckline curve (see page 87). Press the seam allowances towards the facing and understitch (see page 83) the facing from the right side. Be sure to only stitch through the facing and the seam allowance.

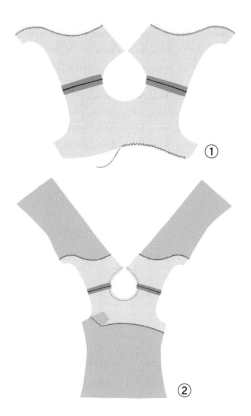

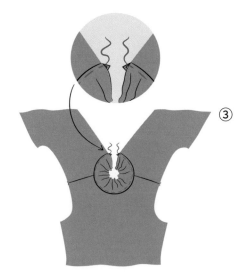

4   Now turn the facing inside out, so that the facing and garment are right sides together. Pin the facing around the armholes and the centre back neck opening, matching the shoulder seams. Machine stitch in place. Clip into the curved armhole seams.

5   Attach a safety pin to one corner of each back piece. Use the safety pin the slide the first back piece through the 'tunnel' at the shoulder, through to the right side. Repeat on the opposite shoulder.

6   From the wrong side, press the facing really flat at the armholes, centre back opening and neckline, rolling the seamlines in towards the wrong side as you press.

7   Place the front and back of the garment right sides together, matching the side seams. Lift up the facing at the side seams and pin and stitch the side seams from the top of the facing through the underarm seam, all the way down to the hem. Press the seams open and turn the facing to the wrong side of the garment. Press the armhole edge. Use a hand stitch to secure the hem of the facing to the side seams.

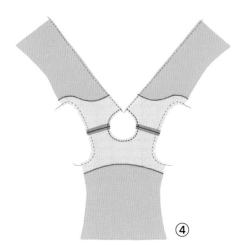

④

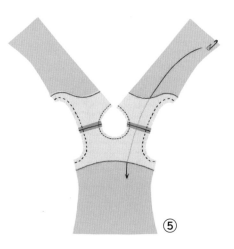

⑤

⑦

8 Pin and sew the centre back seam from the hem to the bottom of the facing. Press the seam open. Insert the fastening of your choice into the centre back seam.

....

TIPS

- A facing should be exactly the same shape as the garment edge that it finishes, so if you alter the shape of the garment in any way (for example, by changing the shape of the neckline), remember to alter the facing to match.

- Facings are usually interfaced. Choose an interfacing that's the same weight or lighter than the garment fabric.

....

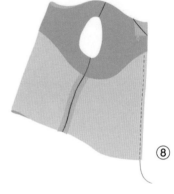

⑧

WAIST FINISHES

Waist finishes fall into two broad categories: fixed waist finishes, which include waistbands and waist facings, and casings, which are channels that enclose elastic or a drawstring to pull the fabric in around the waist.

STRAIGHT WAISTBAND

Straight waistbands extend beyond the waist edge at one end, so that you can attach a fastening, such as a button and buttonhole or hooks and eyes. Sew the side seams and attach any zip (zipper) to the garment before you sew on the waistband.

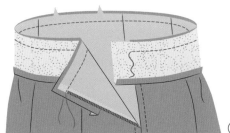

1   If your waistband has a buttonhole, transfer the marking from the pattern to the right side of the fabric. Apply interfacing to the wrong side of the waistband (see page 72). Once it is cool, turn under the seam allowance on the long, un-notched edge of the waistband and press. Trim the seam allowance on this pressed-under edge to 1 cm (⅜ in.).

2   With right sides together, matching the notches on the waistband with the notches or seams on the garment, pin the waistband to the upper edge of the garment. (Note that the front will be longer than the back.) Stitch in place, trim the seam allowance and press the seam towards the waistband.

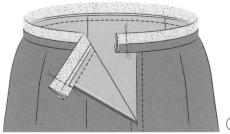

3   With right sides together, fold the waistband in half widthways. Stitch across the short ends and trim the seam allowance.

4 Turn the waistband right side out and carefully push the ends out to get crisp, sharp corners. Press. The long edge of the waistband that you pressed under in step 1 will just cover the waistline seam; slipstitch (see page 82) this edge over the seam and slipstitch the extension edges together.

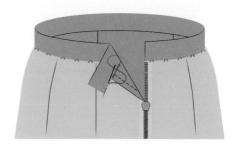

④

....

TIP

As an alternative to slipstitching the long edge of the waistband in step 4, you can 'stitch in the ditch' (see page 156) from the right side.

....

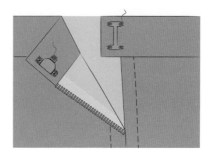

⑤

5 Stitch a buttonhole (see page 102) or sew a hook (see page 107) in the overlap end of the waistband, then attach a button or a bar to the other end of the waistband to correspond.

WAIST FACING

Facings are shaped sections of fabrics that finish off the raw edges of clothes at the neckline, waist, armholes and even hems. Once attached, a facing is turned to the inside of a garment, so is invisible from the outside. Waist facings add stability around the curved waistline and stop them from stretching over time.

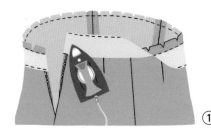

1. Apply interfacing to the wrong side of the waist facing. Open up the zip (zipper) on the garment. With right sides together, pin the facing to the garment around the waistline, matching up the side seams and matching the back darts with the corresponding notches on the facing. Stitch in place. Clip into the seam allowance around the waist. Press the facing and seam allowances away from the waistline.

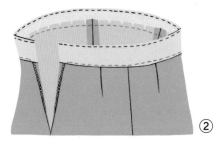

2. Understitch all around the facing, just below the seam line at the waist (see page 83); you're stitching the seam allowance to the facing only. This will stop the facing from rolling out from the inside. Start and end this stitching 2.5 cm (1 in.) away from the zip.

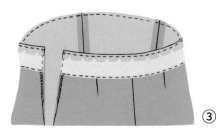

3. Change the regular sewing foot to a zip foot. Line up the short edges of the facing pieces with the seam allowance and pin in place over the zip. Sew in place by stitching close to the zip teeth.

4. Tuck your thumb into the corner at the top of the zip and, folding the layers around your thumb, turn the facing through to the right side, wrapping it over to the wrong side of the garment. Once it's turned through, press to create a really sharp corner and press around the waistline to create a neat top edge.

5. Hand stitch the facing to the right-hand side seam, centre front and centre back of the garment. This will keep the facing on the inside of the garment when worn.

FOLD-DOWN CASINGS

A fold-down casing is made by turning down the waist edge of the garment to form a channel into which elastic or a drawstring is inserted. It is best used on straight edges.

FOLD-DOWN CASING FOR ELASTIC

1 Turn under and press the hem allowance along the top edge of the casing. Turn the top edge under along the waistline and pin in place.

2 Machine stitch along the lower edge of the casing, leaving a gap at the centre back seam for the elastic. Work a second row of stitching all the way around the top edge.

3 Attach a safety pin to one end of the elastic and feed it through the casing, making sure the other end doesn't disappear inside the casing by pinning it to the garment at the start of the gap. Ease the waistline fabric along as you feed the elastic through, then pin the two ends of elastic together.

4 Stitch the ends of the elastic together by stitching around them in a square shape without lifting the needle; this is known as box stitching. Ease the elastic back into the casing.

5 Slipstitch (see page 82) or machine stitch the gap in the bottom edge of the casing closed.

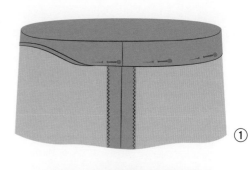

①

②

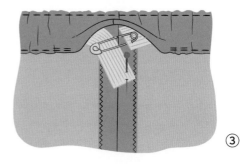

③

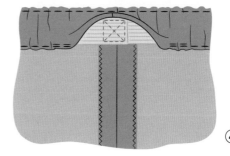

④

TIPS

- To work out how much elastic you need, measure around your waist and deduct 2.5 cm (1 in.) for a snug fit.

- If box stitching (see Fold-down casing for elastic, step 4, page 139) will create too much bulk, stitch the ends of the elastic to a small piece of fabric, butting them up against each other.

- To prevent the elastic from twisting during laundering, stitch vertically down through all thicknesses at the side seams and at the centre back seam, if applicable.

FOLD-DOWN CASING FOR A DRAWSTRING

1 Following the markings on your pattern, make two vertical buttonholes in the casing (this is normally at the centre front of the garment), then follow step 1 of Fold-down casing for elastic (page 139). Machine stitch all the way along the lower edge of the casing, then work a second row of stitching all the way around the top edge.

2 Attach a safety pin to one end of the drawstring. Feed it through one of the buttonholes, all the way around the garment and out of the other buttonhole.

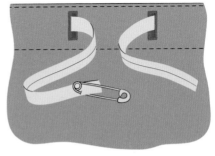

②

APPLIED CASING FOR ELASTIC

An applied casing is created from a separate piece of fabric.

1 To calculate the width of the casing fabric or bias binding, measure the width of the elastic being used and add 12 mm (½ in.) for seam allowances plus 10 mm (⅜ in.) for ease. The casing should be long enough to go around the garment ungathered, plus 3 cm (1¼ in.) to neaten the ends. Cut the casing to this measurement, cutting it on the straight grain if the waistline of the garment is straight and on the bias if it is curved.

2 Turn one long edge of the casing to the wrong side by 6 mm (¼ in.) and press. Press 1 cm (⅜ in.) to the wrong side at each short end and machine stitch.

3 Trim the garment waist seam allowance to 1 cm (⅜ in.) With right sides together, starting near a seam, pin the un-pressed edge of the casing all the way around. Stitch in place.

4 Press, then flip the casing to the wrong side of the garment. Pin and stitch the lower edge of the casing in place.

5 Insert the elastic following steps 3 and 4 of Fold-down casing for elastic (page 139). Slipstitch (see page 82) the edges of the casing together, making sure you don't catch the elastic in the stitching.

PLEATS AND TUCKS

The terms 'pleat' and 'tuck' are sometimes used interchangeably, but they are different things. Pleats are used to create volume and wearing ease in a garment. They are practical as well as decorative, as they allow for freedom of movement, and they are sewn only across the top to hold them in place. Tucks are usually very narrow and are sewn down their entire length; they are decorative rather than functional. Both, however, require more fabric than normal.

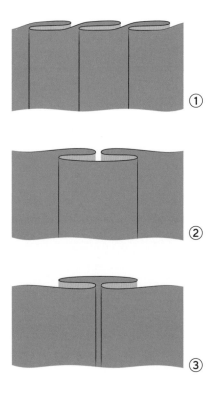

PLEATS

Pleats are a way of adding and controlling volume in a garment. You will often find them around the waist on blouses, dresses, skirts and trousers (pants). The method used determines how much volume you can add.

Knife pleats (1)

Knife pleats are equal folds on the inside and the outside, all facing in the same direction.

Box pleats (2)

Box pleats consist of two knife pleats that face away from each other. The volume sits on the outside of this pleat.

Inverted box pleats (3)

These are the same as box pleats, but in reverse: the two knife pleats face towards each other. The volume sits on the inside of this pleat.

TIP

To ensure that multiple pleats are even, use a pleat template, which is easy to make from a strip of card. Having determined the width of the fabric to be taken in the pleat, cut a card strip to this width. On one long edge, mark 'Placement Line'; on the other long edge, mark 'Fold Line'. Place the card on the right side of the fabric to be pleated and mark the two lines, using a different colour for each.

CONSTRUCTING PLEATS

1 Pleat lines on your pattern are indicated by two lines and an arrow for the direction in which to fold the pleat. The line that the arrow is pointing to is called the Placement Line; the other line is the Fold Line. Fold the fabric at the Fold Line mark and bring it to the Placement Line mark, keeping the raw edges of the fabric even. The pleat formed will be half the width of the marked fabric.

2 For pleats that are functional rather than decorative (like a waist pleat), the pleats are only pinned and pressed right at the edge, so they can be sewn into the seam. We recommend machine tacking (basting) them down within the seam allowance. The rest of the pleat creates volume in the garment. Some garments have pleats along the entire length of the garment for decoration and volume (like a pleated skirt), in which case you press the entire pleat to make it lie flat.

PATTERN MARKINGS FOR A KNIFE PLEAT

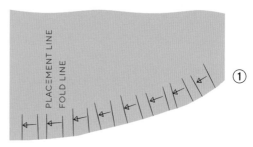

PATTERN MARKINGS FOR A BOX PLEAT

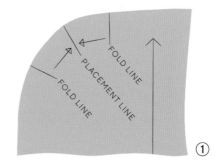

3   Machine tack across the top of the pleats to hold them in place, tacking within the seam allowance. You can also stitch down the 2–3 cm (1 in. or so) of the pleat to create a flatter shape; to do this, stitch very close to the folded edge of the pleat.

4   To keep pleats folded in place, working from the wrong side, machine stitch close to the inner fold, particularly in the hem area.

5   Press your pleats very carefully if you are pressing them in! Place a pressing cloth in between the iron and the garment to prevent the pleat indentations showing on the garment.

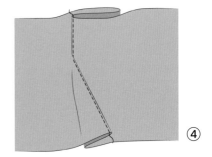

PIN TUCKS

Narrow pin tucks create a subtle surface detail that adds a distinct designer feel to a garment. Often used on heirloom garments, especially children's clothes and christening gowns, they also look smart on crisp, formal shirts and blouses. They are most effective when stitched in multiple pin-tuck groups.

TWIN NEEDLE PIN TUCKS

1   Insert a twin needle with gap of 2 mm (⅛ in.). Select a straight stitch, with the needle in the centre position. Increase the top tension to the highest (7–9) and use a stitch length of 2. Attach the pin tuck foot. Thread the machine for twin needle sewing, following the instructions in your sewing machine manual.

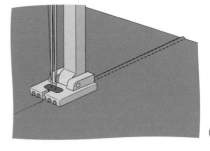

2   Mark the fabric for the placement of the first row of pin tucks. Stitch the first row with the centre of the pin tuck foot on the marked line.

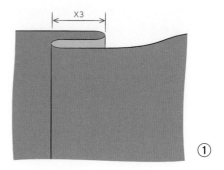

3   Having stitched the first tuck, move the fabric so that the first tuck runs in one of the grooves on either side of the centre of the foot, so that the next tuck is perfectly parallel to the first. Stitch all the tucks in the same direction.

SEWING PIN TUCKS WITHOUT A SPECIALIST FOOT OR TWIN NEEDLE

Pin tucks can be sewn without specialist tools – you just need to take more care in marking the tuck positions and ensure they are stitched accurately.

If you are using a commercial pattern, the tucks will be marked on the pattern pieces. Transfer these markings to the right side of the fabric at the seam edge, using a different pin or chalk colour to determine which is the fold line and which is the stitching line.

1   If you are making your own, determine the depth of the finished tuck and multiply by three. Also allow a gap between tucks – the width is up to you. With these two measurements added together, mark the fold lines on the fabric at top and bottom by snipping into the seam allowance or using pins.

2   Fold the fabric along the fold line from top to bottom, with wrong sides together, and press carefully to make a firm crease.

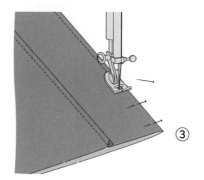

3   Place the fabric under the presser foot, and stitch a straight line the tuck depth required from the fold.

4   Unfold the tucked fabric and then refold to stitch the next tuck in the same manner. Always press in the fold first to make sure that they are stitched in straight rows.

SHIRRING

Shirring is a really easy technique that gives a lovely smocked effect on fabric. It's important to make up the shirred panel before you assemble your garment, so that you can make sure it's the exact size you need. Mark your shirring lines really carefully before you start. You need a sewing machine, elastic sewing thread for the bobbin and regular thread for the needle.

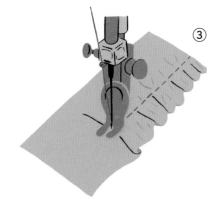

1   Wind your bobbin with the elastic thread by hand: aim for a little bit of tension when you do this, without fully using the elasticity of the thread. Distribute the thread evenly around the bobbin, and set up the rest of your machine as usual.

2   Lower the needle tension on your machine and do a sample stitch: you should see the elastic bobbin thread on the back and only the needle thread on the front.

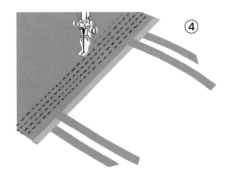

3   Start your first line, and don't backstitch. After a few stitches, tie up the needle and bobbin threads by hand at the start of your line. When you reach the end of your first line, tie the thread ends by hand again instead of backstitching.

4   Sew all subsequent rows by pulling the fabric flat, to achieve even lines.

TIPS

- If your stitches are not gathering and the elastic looks loose on the back: change your bobbin tension.

- If the needle thread looks as if it's only looping around the elastic on the back: change your needle tension.

- If you are sewing lots of rows, check your bobbin thread regularly, as the elastic thread will run out much quicker than you think! You won't be able to restart halfway through a line of stitching once the bobbin thread has run out.

- When you finish sewing each row, be sure to pull the elastic thread a long way out. If you cut it too close to the fabric, it may ping back inside the bobbin and unthread.

WHAT'S THE DIFFERENCE BETWEEN SHIRRING AND SMOCKING?

Both are decorative gathering techniques that are used to control fullness in a garment. Smocking is traditionally done by hand, using stranded cotton embroidery thread (floss); the fabric is first gathered evenly into precisely measured and marked folds, then embroidery stitches are worked over the top to create a decorative effect. Shirring is done by machine and involves sewing parallel rows across the fabric, with elastic thread on the bobbin and regular sewing thread in the needle.

BIAS BINDING

Bias binding not only finishes the edges of a garment beautifully but also neatly encases the raw edges. Bound edges look great on necklines, sleeveless armholes and edge-to-edge jackets. They are ideal on garments where the reverse will show, as the edges are neat and uniform, and on transparent fabrics where any facings would show through.

Bindings are usually made from bias-cut strips of fabric, so that they will bend around curved areas easily and without ripples. You can buy bias binding ready cut and with the edges pressed in. It comes in a variety of widths and endless colours. Alternatively, you can make your own, either in the same fabric as the garment or as a contrast trim.

Calculating the width of the binding strip

Work out the width of the binding you want to see on the edge of a garment. To achieve a visible width of 1 cm (⅜ in.), which is a nice width in dressmaking, double the visible width required and add 12 mm (½ in.) for seam allowances – so you would need strips 32 mm (1¼ in.) wide. With the long edges turned in by 6 mm (¼ in.), the tape would be 2 cm (¾ in.) – and thus 1 cm (⅜ in.) wide when folded over a seam.

MAKING YOUR OWN BIAS BINDING

1   To find the bias, pull out a crossways (weft) thread (one that runs from selvedge to selvedge) near the raw edge

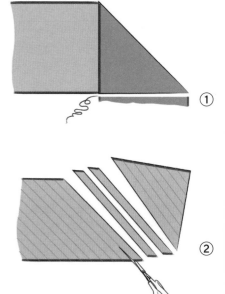

①

②

of the fabric (see page 63). Cut along the line created by the pulled thread. Fold this straight edge diagonally until it matches the selvedge. Press along the fold. This diagonal line is the bias. Cut along the line.

2   Using a steel ruler and tailor's chalk, measure out and mark the desired width of the binding at regular intervals along the diagonal line. Cut along the lines using dressmaker's scissors or a rotary cutter and cutting mat.

3 Pin the cut lengths end to end with right sides together along the selvedge or crossways grain. This will form a V shape. Stitch and then press the seams open.

4 Once you have made up the length you need, trim off the protruding ends of the seams and press in a 6 mm (¼ in) hem to the wrong side along each long edge.

APPLYING BIAS BINDING

1 Unfold one long edge and place it with right sides together along the edge you plan to bind. Pin and then stitch it in place along the crease line. Trim the seam to 6 mm (¼ in).

2 **Revealed method**
To use bias binding as a trim, fold the bias binding over the seam allowance to the wrong side and pin and tack (baste) in place. Topstitch from the right side (see page 83), then remove the tacking stitches.

3 **Concealed method**
With this method, the binding is visible only on the inside of the bound edge. It is suitable for necklines and armholes and functions as a mini facing (see page 131). Trim the seam allowance, then fold the whole width of the bias binding to the wrong side. The stitch line joining the bias binding to the main piece will lie exactly on the edge of the garment when it is finished. Topstitch in place (see page 83).

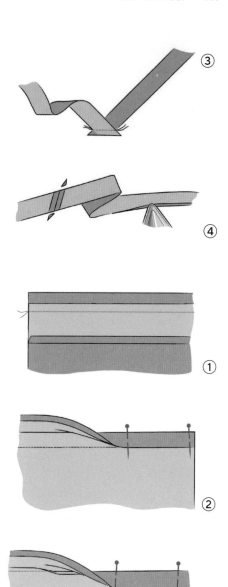

OVERLAPPING ENDS

If the binding ends will meet, the ends need to be overlapped as inconspicuously as possible.

1 Turn the raw end of the start of the bias binding to the wrong side and press. Pin this end to the garment, with the long edge unfolded and raw edges even, and follow step 1 on page 149. When you reach the end, allow the unneatened end to overlap the turned start by approximately 1 cm (⅜ in.) and stitch down. When you fold the binding over to the wrong side of the garment, the neatened end will be uppermost.

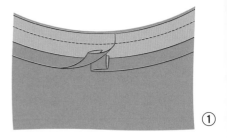
①

GOING AROUND CORNERS

You can start each edge separately and then slipstitch(see page 82) the ends together over the edge, or you can fold and turn the binding, which is a neater finish.

1 Mark the seam lines at the corners on the fabric. Stitch the first section of binding to the garment edge as above, ending the stitching where the seams intersect at the corner. Reverse stitch a few stitches, then cut the thread.

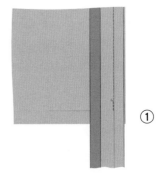
①

2 Fold the binding to the right and create a diagonal crease.

3 Keeping the crease in place, fold the binding again so that the tape is now along the next edge, ready to be sewn in place.

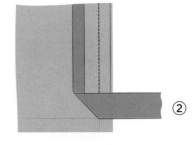
②

4 Keeping the folded triangle of tape out of the way, carefully insert the needle into the corner intersection point and continue stitching to the next corner. Repeat for each corner.

③

5 Turn the binding to the wrong side as before, making a diagonal fold in the corner. Slipstitch in place, stitching the mitred corner as well if desired.

SEWING ON BINDING WITH JUST ONE SEAM

With this method, you can stitch your bias binding on with only one stitch line! As the binding is visible on both sides of the bound edge, this technique is suitable for decorative binding and for finishing seam allowances that are visible.

1 If you are making binding yourself, fold the long raw edges of your bias strip in to the centre (this is how it arrives if you buy it ready made). Then fold the bias binding in half lengthways, wrong sides together, with a step: one side should be about 3 mm (⅛ in.) wider than the other. Press well.

2 Slot the binding around the raw edge that you are binding. The wider half should lie underneath. Topstitch from the right side; you will automatically catch the other side of the binding in the stitches, as it's a little bit wider.

TIPS

° Making your own bias binding means you can match or contrast with your main fabric of the garment, giving you more choice of colourways and patterns.

° If you are making your own binding, check that the fabric you use is compatible with your main fabric in both weight and laundering needs.

° When buying bias binding, note that the width quoted is the width of the tape with the long edges already folded inside.

° A bias binding tape maker is a handy gadget to add to your sewing kit. All you have to do is pull your bias-cut strip through it, pressing with an iron as you go; it will turn under the edges for you, eliminating the need to measure and fold. It takes a bit of practice to get the pressure and angle right, but if you're likely to be making a lot of bias binding, it's a really worthwhile investment. Tape makers come in various widths; one that makes a 2.5-cm (1-in.) binding is probably the most useful.

° It's a good idea to staystitch any curves (see page 83) before you apply bias binding to prevent them from stretching out of shape.

FREE-HANGING LINING

Adding a free-hanging lining can improve the way a garment hangs, reduce creasing, and prevent bagging at the seat and knees in dresses, skirts and trousers (pants). Lining pieces are usually cut from the same pattern pieces as the main garment, omitting the waistband, collar or facings. This method involves stitching the garment and lining together at the top (waist or neckline) and sometimes the front edges. The garment and lining are hemmed separately.

LINING A SKIRT OR TROUSERS (PANTS)

1 Cut the lining from the same pattern pieces as the garment, excluding the waistband.

2 Make up the main fabric garment, except for the waistband and hem.

3 Make up the lining garment, leaving an opening for the zip (zipper) 2.5 cm (1 in.) longer than in the garment. Press the seams open and the waist darts away from the centre.

4 With wrong sides together, matching the darts, centres and side seams and aligning the raw edges at the waistline, pin the lining to the garment. Turn under the edges of the lining along the zip tape and slipstitch to the tape.

5 Machine baste the waistline edges together 13 mm (½ in.) from the edge. Following the pattern instructions, sew the waistband or facing to the garment.

④

⑥

6 Hem the garment first (see page 88), then make the lining hem approximately 13 mm (½ in.) shorter than the garment hem. (The lining hem can be a machine-stitched hem.)

LINING A DRESS

1 Follow steps 1 to 4 of the method for lining a skirt or trousers (pants), slipstitching the lining to the unfinished neckline and armholes of the main fabric dress (see page 82).

FOR A SLEEVELESS DRESS

2 Following the pattern instructions, attach the armhole facings.

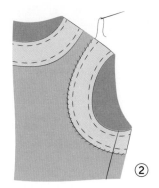

SLEEVELESS DRESS

FOR A DRESS WITH SLEEVES

2 Following the pattern instructions, attach the main fabric sleeve to the main fabric dress.

3 Sew the sleeve lining underarm seam, press the seam open, and turn right side out. With wrong sides together, matching the markings, pin the sleeve lining to the sleeve of the dress. Turn under the seam allowance on the lining sleeve head and hand slipstitch it over the armhole seam.

4 Trim the sleeve lining level with the lower edge of the sleeve. Turn under 13 mm (½ in.) on the sleeve lining and slipstitch it over the sleeve hem.

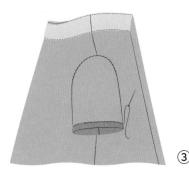

DRESS WITH SLEEVES

TIPS

- A favourite lining fabric for dressmakers is an anti-static lining that allows the body to breathe; it is lightweight, so it doesn't change the drape of the garment. Another option is a fine cotton lawn, which has the same properties as other cotton fabrics and comes in a good range of colours.

- Make sure the lining fabric is a lighter weight – or at least no heavier – than the main fabric

- Make sure the lining fabric and main garment fabric can be laundered in the same way. If the lining fabric is dry clean only and the outer fabric of a garment is machine washable, for example, then the entire garment will need to be dry cleaned each time it is dirty.

GLOSSARY

BASTING

Another word for tacking.

BIAS

On fabric, this runs diagonally across the grain at 45 degrees to the selvedges. The bias of the fabric has the most 'give' and is the most stretchy. *See also* Grain and Selvedges.

BINDING

A narrow strip of fabric wrapped around an edge of a garment, to enclose the edge and also for decorative purposes. Bias binding is made from fabric cut on the bias.

CASING

A channel, usually at the waist or neckline of a garment, through which elastic or a drawstring can be threaded.

DART

A fold (often triangular or diamond-shaped) sewn into the cut-out fabric to give the garment a three-dimensional shape to fit the contours of the body. Darts may be single (V-shaped) or contour (tapering to a point at each end); contour darts are also known as double-ended or fish-eye darts.

DIRECTIONAL PRINT

A fabric in which the design clearly faces or goes in one direction. Such fabrics need to be cut with all the pieces facing in the same direction, otherwise the design will be upside down on some pieces.

DRAPE

The way a fabric falls in folds.

EASE

The difference between the finished garment measurement and the body measurement, which means that the garment is not skin tight and the wearer has room to move. For example, on a dress pattern designed for someone with a 98-cm (38½-in.) bust, the finished garment bust measurement might be 116 cm (45½ in.); the pattern therefore has 18 cm (7 in.) ease.

EASE STITCHING

Slightly longer-than-normal machine stitches that are then gathered to fit a longer edge of fabric into a shorter one. Ease stitching is used to attach set-in sleeves, join princess-seamed pieces and take up hems on circular skirts without leaving ripples.

EDGE STITCHING

The same as topstitching, but sewn much closer to the edge, hence its name. It is meant to be visible on the surface of the fabric. *See also* Topstitching.

FACING

A piece of fabric used to neaten the edges on armholes, necklines and waists, as well as the front openings of some garments. Facings are cut to the same shape as the area of the garment to which they are attached and interfaced to add support. Once sewn into position, they are folded to the inside to create a neat outside edge.

FEED DOGS

Metal teeth-like ridges that rotate to move the fabric on under the presser foot as you sew.

FINISHING

Ways of neatening the raw edges on the inside of seams.

GATHERING

Gathering can be done by hand or by machine. On a machine, stitch just inside the seamline, leaving long thread tails at each end, then pull up the bobbin thread from each end to gather the fabric. By hand, use double thread and take long running stitches, pulling up the fabric as required.

GRADING

Cutting the seam allowances to different depths to reduce bulk.

GRAIN

The threads in the fabric, running either horizontally or vertically. The straight of grain, or lengthwise grain, runs parallel to the selvedge and does not have any stretch. The cross grain, or crosswise grain, runs between the selvedges and stretches slightly. *See also* Bias.

GRAINLINE

Most pattern pieces have grainlines marked on them, which need to be aligned parallel to the selvedges on the 'straight of grain' to prevent the garment pieces from twisting and hanging lopsided.

INTERFACING

A type of fabric that is added to the reverse of some areas in a garment in order to add body and support. Areas that need to be interfaced include buttonholes, waistbands, front facings, collars and cuffs. Interfacings may be either fusible (iron-on) or sew-in and come in different weights.

LAY PLAN

A diagram included in a commercial pattern that shows you how to position the paper pattern pieces on the fabric in the most economical way and in what orientation.

NAP

This is the pile element on fabrics such as velvet, corduroy, velour or velveteen that is woven into the material during the construction process. It also refers to fabrics printed with a one-way or directional design. Commercial patterns usually have 'with nap' lay plans.

NOTCH

A triangular symbol on a pattern that is used to match up one pattern piece with another – for example, front to back, sleeves to armholes.

NOTIONS

Another word for haberdashery, notions are all the things other than fabric that you need to make a particular garment – threads, zips (zippers) and other fastenings, decorative trims and so on.

RAW EDGES

Any un-neatened fabric edge other than a selvedge.

RIGHT SIDE/WRONG SIDE

Fabrics have a 'right' side, which is the side that will be visible as the outside of the garment, and a 'wrong' side, which is the reverse. If the fabric is a solid colour and it is difficult to tell the right side from the wrong, mark each piece that you cut with a chalk cross on the wrong side, so that you put the pieces together accurately. Sometimes a very slight shade variance may be visible in daylight.

SEAM ALLOWANCE

The distance between the stitching and the fabric edge; in dressmaking this is generally 1.5 cm (⅝ in.), but always follow your pattern instructions.

SELVEDGES

The side edges of the fabric, parallel to the straight of grain (lengthwise grain). They are often woven slightly tighter than the rest of the fabric, so they should not be included when you cut out a pattern piece. The selvedges do not fray or unravel.

STAYSTITCHING

Straight machine stitching worked just inside the seam allowance on curved or bias-cut edges to prevent them from stretching while the garment is being constructed.

STITCHING IN THE DITCH

Stitching done directly on top of a previous seamline, from the right side of the garment. Done well, the stitching disappears inside the crease (or 'ditch') of the seam.

TACKING

Long, temporary stitches used to hold pieces of fabric together. You can tack by hand or machine – on a machine, set the stitch length to the longest possible so that it will be easy to remove later.

THROAT PLATE

The metal plate on the sewing machine underneath the needle and presser foot. It incorporates a hole for the needle and the feed dogs. *See also* Feed dogs.

TOILE

A mock-up of a garment in a plain fabric such as calico that you can make any fit adjustments to before you cut into your expensive garment fabric.

TOPSTITCHING

A line of stitches worked on the outside of a garment. This may be either for functional reasons, such as holding a facing in place, or for a decorative finish.

UNDERSTITCHING

This is done to anchor the seam allowance to a facing, which helps prevent the facing from rolling out after it has been turned to the inside of the garment.

INDEX

altering patterns 44–54
armhole facings 132–5

back: altering patterns 51
  measurements 41
belts 108–9
bias 154
bias binding 148–51, 154
biceps, measurements 41
blind hemming 90–1
bobbins, filling with thread 76
box pleats 142–3
bulk, reducing 87
bust: altering patterns 48–50
  darts 47, 93
  measurements 41
  pattern sizes 43
buttonholes 102–4
buttons 102, 104, 105–6, 110
buying fabrics 22–3

carbon paper, dressmaker's 68
casings 154
  applied 141
  fold-down 139–40
  sleeve finishes 116
catch stitch 82
circles, on patterns 61
collars 127–30
contour darts 93
corners: reducing bulk 87
  sewing seams 78
cotton fabrics 25
covered buttons 106
crotch depth, altering patterns
  52–3
cuffs 41, 117–20
curved hems 90
curved seams 85
cutting fabrics 66–7
cutting lines, on patterns 61
cutting tools 13

darts 92–3, 154
  altering patterns 47–50
  bust darts 47, 93

pattern markings 61
diagonal tacking 81
directional prints 154
drape, fabrics 22, 154
drawstrings, casings 140
dresses: linings 153
  sizes 43
dressmaker's carbon paper 68

ease 45, 154
easing/ease stitch 83, 154
edge stitching 83, 86, 154
elastic: casings 139–41
  shirring 146–7
  sleeve hems 115–16
equipment 10–19

fabric ties 108–9
fabrics 20–37
  cutting 66–7
  grain 62–3
  nap 65, 155
  pattern matching 70–1
  pinning patterns to 66
  pressing 59
  pretreating 58–9
  widths 23
facings 131–5, 155
  armhole facings 132–5
  neck facings 131, 133–5
  waist facings 138
fastenings 94–110
  buttons and buttonholes 102–6
  fabric ties 108–9
  hooks 107
  no-sew fastenings 110
  press studs 110
  zips 94–101
feed dogs, sewing machines
  155
fell stitch 82
finishing seams 86, 155
fitting guidelines, patterns 45
flat collars 127–8
flat fell seams 84
fly zips 100–1

fold-down casings 139–40
French seams 85

gathering stitches 83, 155
grading, reducing seam bulk
  87, 155
grading patterns 43, 44
grain, fabrics 62–3, 155
grainline, on patterns 61, 65, 155

haberdashery 60
hand stitches 81–2
hems 88–91
  blind hemming 90–1
  double-turned hems 89
  full or curved hems 90
  hem allowance 88
  sleeves 115
  twin needle topstitched hem 89
herringbone stitch 82
hip pockets 126
hips: measurements 41
  pattern sizes 43
hooks 107
horizontal pinning, seams 80

interfacing 72–3, 155
interlining 155
invisible zips 98–9
iron-on (fusible) interfacing
  72, 73

jackets, sizes 43
jeans buttons 110

knife pleats 142–3
knit (stretch) fabrics 28–9
knitted interfacing 72

lace 30
lay plans, patterns 64–5, 155
leg measurements 41
lengthening patterns 46
linen fabrics 25
lines, on patterns 61
linings 152–3

luxury fabrics 30–3

marking tools 12, 68
markings: on patterns 60–1
  transferring pattern markings
  68–9
measurements 40–2
measuring tools 12

nap, fabrics 65, 155
neck: facings 131, 133–5
  measurements 41
needles, sewing machines 19
no-sew fastenings 110
non-woven interfacing 72
notches 61, 155
  cutting around 67
notching seams 87
notions 60, 156

overlockers 86

patch pockets 122–4
pattern matching, fabrics 70–1
patterns: altering 44–54
  fitting guidelines 45
  lay plans 64–5, 155
  markings and terminology 60–1
  pinning and cutting 66
  sizes 43
  toiles 55
  transferring markings 68–9
  understanding 60–73
pin hemming 91
pin tucks 144–5
pins: pinning patterns 66
  pinning seams 80
  transferring pattern markings 69
placket openings, shirt sleeves
  118
pleats 142–4
pockets 122–6
press studs 110
pressing fabrics 59
pressing tools 14
pretreating fabrics 58–9
printed fabrics, pattern
  matching 70–1

raglan sleeves 113–14
raw edges 156
'repeat', fabrics 70
right side/wrong side 156
rouleau loops 109

satin fabrics 32
seams 84–5
  finishes 86, 155
  in-seam pockets 125
  pinning 80
  reducing bulk 87
  seam allowance 156
  tacking 81
selvedges 156
sequinned fabrics 33
set-in sleeves 112
sew-in interfacing 73
sewing machines 16–19
  blind hemming 90
  buttonholes 103–4
  maintenance 18
  neatening seam allowances 86
  needles 19
  pin hemming 91
  practising 78
  stitch tension 79
  stitches 83
  threading 76–7
sewing tools 13–14
sheer fabrics 31
shirring 146–7
shirt collars 129–30
shirt sleeves 111, 118
shortening patterns 46
shrinkage 58
silk fabrics 27
single darts 92
sizing 43
skirts: linings 152
  sizes 43
slash and spread, altering
  patterns 54
sleeves 111–21
  cuffs 117–20
  finishes 115–16
  measurements 41
  raglan sleeves 113–14
  set-in sleeves 112
  sleeve tabs 121
  T-shirt and shirt sleeves 111
slipstitch 82
smocking 147
stand (shirt) collars 129–30
staystitching 83, 156
steaming wool 58
stitches: blind hemming 90–1
  hand stitches 81–2
  sewing machines 83
  tension 79

stitching in the ditch 156
straight grain, fabrics 62–3
straight seams 84
stretch (knit) fabrics 28–9

T-shirt sleeves 111
tacking 81, 156
taffeta 32
tailor's chalk 68
tailor's tacks 69
tension, stitch 79
thread: tailor's tacks 69
  threading sewing machines
  76–7
throat plate, sewing machines 156
ties 108–9
toiles 55, 156
tops, sizes 43
topstitching 83, 156
  twin needle topstitched hem 89
tracing wheels 68
transferring pattern markings
  68–9
trims, pretreating 58
trousers: altering patterns 52–3
  fly zips 100–1
  linings 152
  sizes 43
tucks 142, 144–5
twin needle pin tucks 144–5
twin needle topstitched hem 89

understitching 83, 156

vertical pinning, seams 80
vertical stitch 82

waist: altering darts 47
  casings for elastic 139–41
  facings 138
  finishes 136–41
  measurements 41
  pattern sizes 43
  straight waistbands 136–7
washing, prewashing fabrics 58
weighting down pattern pieces
  66
wool fabrics 26, 58
woven fabrics 24–7
woven interfacing 72

zigzag stitch 86
zips 94–101

ACKNOWLEDGEMENTS

Some of the content of this book has appeared in previous *The Great British Sewing Bee* publications and our thanks go to their authors – Caroline Akselson, Alexandra Bruce, Tessa Evelegh, Wendy Gardiner and Claire-Louise Hardie – all of whom are as passionate about sewing as they are knowledgeable, and unfailingly generous in sharing their expertise. We would like to thank the judges, Patrick Grant, Esme Young and May Martin, for their keen eye and attention to detail. Thanks, too, to Steven Dew, Suzie London and Kate Simunek for their wonderfully clear step-by-step illustrations. New text for this book was provided by Sarah Hoggett. At Quadrille, the dream team of Senior Commissioning Editor Harriet Butt and Senior Designer Emily Lapworth have – as always – brought their exemplary organizational skills and creative flair to the project.

Of course, none of this would be possible without the team at Love Productions, who create and produce all *The Great British Sewing Bee* programmes. As viewers, we see the warmth and enthusiasm of the judges and presenters as they steer the contestants through the various sewing challenges. Behind the scenes, however, there's a whole army of people too numerous to list individually, writing and checking patterns, sourcing fabrics, fixing sewing machines when they break down, and generally making everything run like clockwork. Our thanks to all of them for their hard work and dedication and allowing us into the fabulous, fun- and fabric-filled workroom of *The Great British Sewing Bee*.

This book is a compilation of the books published to accompany the television series entitled *The Great British Sewing Bee*. The Great British Sewing Bee is a registered trademark of Love Productions Ltd.

Executive Producer Sara Ramsden
Series Producer Catherine Lewendon
Sewing Producer Sue Suma
Director of Legal & Commercial Affairs
Rupert Frisby

Quadrille, Penguin Random House UK, One Embassy Gardens, 8 Viaduct Gardens, London SW11 7BW

Quadrille Publishing Limited is part of the Penguin Random House group of companies whose addresses can be found at global. penguinrandomhouse.com

Penguin
Random House
UK

Text © Love Productions 2021
Photography © Clare Nicolson 2021
Cover illustrations © Debbie Powell 2021
Design, illustrations and layout ©
Quadrille Publishing Ltd 2021

Love Productions has asserted their right to be identified as the author of this Work in accordance with the Copyright, Designs and Patents Act 1988

Published by Quadrille in 2021

www.penguin.co.uk

A CIP catalogue record for this book is available from the British Library

ISBN 978 1 78713 755 4

10 9

Publishing Director Sarah Lavelle
Senior Commissioning Editor Harriet Butt
Project Editor Sarah Hoggett
Art Director & Designer Emily Lapworth
Photographer & Stylist Clare Nicolson
Cover Illustrator Debbie Powell
Technical Illustrators Suzie London, Kate Simunek and Steven Dew
Head of Production Stephen Lang
Production Controller Katie Jarvis

Colour reproduction by F1

Printed in China by C&C Offset Printing Co., Ltd.

The authorised representative in the EEA is Penguin Random House Ireland, Morrison Chambers, 32 Nassau Street, Dublin D02 YH68.

Penguin Random House is committed to a sustainable future for our business, our readers and our planet. This book is made from Forest Stewardship Council® certified paper.